CW00446654

THE PENSION TRUSTEE'S HANDBOOK

Third edition

The definitive guide to practical pension fund trusteeship

Robin Ellison

THOROGOOD

Third edition printed by Thorogood 2003
10-12 Rivington Street, London EC2A 3DU
Telephone: 020 7749 4748

Fax: 020 7729 6110
Email: info@thorogood.ws
Web: www.thorogood.ws

A catalogue record for this book is available
from the British Library

ISBN 1-85418-022-3

Printed in India by Replika Press Pvt. Ltd.

CONTENTS

FOREWORD
PREFACE

PART 1
TRUSTEESHIP IN LAW

PART II
TRUSTEESHIP IN PRACTICE

PART III
BLUFFER'S GUIDE

FOREWORD
PREFACE

PART I
TRUSTEESHIP IN LAW

PART II
TRUSTEESHIP IN PRACTICE

PART III
THE BLUFFER'S GUIDE

FOREWORD

Over the last ten years the obligations of trustees have been widely extended; first the Pensions Act 1995 imposed new duties, then the Occupational Pensions Regulatory Authority and the Pensions Ombudsman began to impose penalties and later the Myners inquiry recommended an extension of responsibilities in relation to investments.

So individuals who accept the demanding but worthwhile office of trustee need to know what they have taken on – and how to cope with the issues that arise from time to time. Many trustees will need access to appropriate training, but they also need a handy, up-to-date practical guide to refer to.

This third edition of Robin Ellison's 'Pension Trustees' Handbook' provides every trustee with a guide, not only written in direct and accessible language but also based on the author's years of practical experience as a pensions lawyer and trustee.

NAPF has long campaigned for pension simplification. While the Government seems at last to recognise the need for this, it will be some years before we can move to a simpler pensions regime. As Robin Ellison states 'pensions complexity is such that few understand the detail'. The direct language and structure of the Handbook distinguishes the basic obligations and responsibilities from some of the more peripheral issues. With this book at their side, the pension trustees have a good chance of being well informed.

The NAPF believes that the present burden of regulation surrounding the operation of occupational pension schemes is too great. Reforms have been suggested in recent years, but we know there is a great deal more to be done in reduce the present over-detailed and counter-productive regulation of schemes. What still matters most is the basic principles of trust law under which trustees hold the money for the benefit of others supported by a wise and alert body of trustees, which has proved balanced and effective for over eighty years. To help trustees in their decision making, a book such as this is an essential tool.

Christine Farnish
Chief Executive, National Association of Pension Funds, 2003

PREFACE

This book was written to meet the practical needs of trustees of pension funds. It is based on many years of experience of teaching and lecturing to pension fund trustees, and sitting on the boards of trustees of pension funds, as well as advising as a solicitor.

It tries to answer the questions most frequently asked by trustees coming fresh to the field, in a non-technical way. It has been read and commented on by colleagues in practice and by trustees both professional and lay, and by pension managers, for whose help and advice I am grateful.

The book is also designed to respond to many of the questions that emerged following the Pensions Act 1995 and the stream of regulations, still being amended some seven years later, which followed, and anticipate changes presaged in the 2002 DWP Green Paper. The Maxwell scandal, a decade ago the catalyst for a review of trustees duties, has now been overtaken by a wide range of events that threaten the very existence of the occupational pensions. It is designed to be read in conjunction with the guide issued by the Occupational Pensions Regulatory Authority, itself shortly to be replaced by another kind of regulator.

If you have any suggestions for improvement, please let us know and we will do our best to incorporate them in any future edition.

Robin Ellison, 2003

1

PART I

TRUSTEESHIP IN LAW

INTRODUCTION

The arguments against the non-contributory principle....

1   The cost of non-contributory pensions would be enormous...The present British system of non-contributory pensions cost about $40,000,000 for the first year....

2   The non-contributory scheme is unjust in principle. It involves taxation for the rich for the benefit of the poor. It is class legislation...

3   The effect on individual character would be debilitating; the non-contributory scheme puts a premium on thriftlessness. Its adoption would be disastrous to the voluntary agencies for the encouragement of saving...

4   The effect on the family would be disintegrating. It would cause children to withdraw the support which they now give to aged parents. There would follow a general loosening and breaking of family ties....

5   The grant of gratuitous subsidies to aged members of the working class would tend to lower the rate of wages. This would follow not merely through the direct competition of pensioned workers, who would be able to underbid the prevailing rate in the occupations in which they were engaged, but through the indirect influence of the prospect of a subsidy in old age, which would lead workers to accept less in regular wages than they would otherwise be disposed to demand...

Report of the Commission of Old Age Pensions,
Annuities and Insurance, Massachusetts, 1910

Background

You are a trustee. Responsible for a pension fund, perhaps worth quite a lot of money, the money which represents the security and peace of mind of people looking forward to retirement. And potentially liable to fines, disqualification and jail for breach of any of 200 requirements of the Pensions Act 1995.

To have so many other human beings resting their hopes and expectations on you, and to stay awake at night worrying about the potential penalties for breach, could be intimidating. But in fact, most trustees just get on with it. In practice, despite portentous warnings from lawyers and others, the ever-present threat of litigation, maverick decisions of the judicial and quasi-judicial authorities, the recent introduction of a raft of penalties for breach of the legislation and the apparent unimaginable complexity, the job is pretty simple – provided you know what the job is. And where difficulties *do* arise, you need not feel ashamed or embarrassed at being a little lost. Even the most professional of trustees find themselves in a quandary from time to time.

The job of a trustee is a *legal* one, not actuarial, managerial or accounting. This book sets out the legal obligations – and how to deal with them in a relatively painless manner. Provided you are honest, sensible and take proper advice, you can do a lot of good – and come to very little harm.

Yours is not a rare position. There are about a quarter of a million schemes, with perhaps on average two trustees in each scheme – so there may be half-a-million pension scheme trustees.

This slim volume explains, simply and practically, just what you are expected to do – and almost as importantly, what not to do. The appendices contain information which you may need to find out the answers to particular problems. In sum, this book is intended as the ultimate bluffer's guide to pension fund trusteeship.

Why the law is involved

The object of a legal system is to give some form of remedy and protection to persons who would otherwise be adversely affected. This is particularly the case in pension funds, where:

- obligations can last for many years,

- complexity is such that few understand the detail,

- the amounts involved are substantial, and

- a few people hold a great deal of money on behalf of many other people.

The value of a pension can and often does exceed the value of someone's house, so the law needed to protect those interests can be seen to be highly necessary. But the law is not perfect in any field, and it has particular problems with pensions.

First, since the growth of pension rights is a relatively recent phenomenon, so is the growth of pensions law. In recent years, a major problem has been to develop a legal system, and help the judges understand a legal structure, designed originally many years ago for very different purposes. The particular legal structure that applies to pension funds has had to cope with the rather odd, from a legal point of view, nature of pension funds. The reason is that the law (trust law) that looks after the interests of scheme members was developed for family trusts and not for pension trusts.

Secondly, many Acts of Parliament apply to pension rights (involving social security, taxation, investment protection and other fields) – and these do not always relate properly to each other. Indeed in some cases they actually conflict.

What is not in this book

This book does not tell you how to run a pension fund. Your job as trustee is non-executive, and is to ensure that the people who do run the fund (the managers, the investment house, the advisers) are doing their job properly. You are supposed to be more of a non-executive director than a 'hands-on' manager.

Accordingly there is very little about:

- Actuarial science, computerisation, management, the skills of communication and the rest. These are jobs which you can and normally should delegate. **A pension fund trustee is not supposed to be an expert**.

- Ancient problems of trust law relating to the administration of family estates, dating back to the times when you could be expected to manage a duke's estate. **A pension fund trustee is not supposed to be a lawyer**.

- Abstruse details of pensions systems, such as contracting-out, preservation, and lower and higher earnings limits. These are properly the province of your advisers. **A pension fund trustee is not expected to be an administrator or benefits consultant**.

- The complexity of a range of laws which were introduced in the decade after a major scandal involving pensions known as the Maxwell Affair. **A pension fund trustee is not (with some exceptions) expected to comply personally with most of the legislation, but must ensure that his advisers do so on his behalf**.

While the legal and administrative details are important, you will in practice delegate most of them. But you need enough knowledge and experience to enable you to ask the right questions of your adviser – and understand the answers.

What is in this book

This book is intended as a handbook for pension fund trustees, probably the most numerous group of trustees today. You and your colleagues collectively manage around £600B of assets – a sum which is growing, subject to the vagaries of the stock market. This is despite attempts by political anarchists, at either end of the political spectrum, to disband one of the most effective, efficient and cost-effective forms of retirement provision ever invented. Nonetheless, pension schemes do have their imperfections, and the main ones are set out in the next chapter.

How to use this book

The book is in three parts:

- Part I gives a basic grounding in the duties of a pension fund trustee. This is considered essential reading; without this, or something like it, it is difficult to understand just what is expected of a trustee;

- Part II looks at some everyday practical problems faced by trustees, and suggests some ideas for dealing with them;

- Part III gives sources of further information.

Finally, the best way to use this book is not to try to read it from cover to cover, but to dip into it from time to time.

With this volume you should feel free from fear and intimidation, and have knowledge enough to manage the job of pension fund trustee. If you disagree, please write and say so.

2

WHY HAVE A TRUST

Now that almost every soldier who enlisted in the armies of the Union and suffered even from a cold in his head has been pensioned, the Republican party are looking out for some fresh scheme for keeping the surplus under. They seem to have found a pretty substantial one in the Bill which will shortly be introduced into Congress by Mr Connell, of Nebraska. His plan is to pension the emancipated Negroes. Mr Frederick Douglas, the most prominent person of Negro blood in the States, has written a letter warmly supporting the plan. He declares that "the nation has sinned against the Negro, robbed him of the rewards of his labour for a period of two hundred years, and its repentance will not be genuine or complete until, according to the measure of its ability, it shall have made retribution." "There never was," he continues, "and never can be a proposal more just and more beneficent than that contained in your Pension Bill." Apparently, Mr Douglas holds that the Negroes, instead of being merely emancipated, should have been endowed with the means of subsistence, as was the Russian serf, who received three acres of land and farming tools: and he now wants to set this wrong right. The proposal is of course utterly absurd and fantastic, and is not meant to be carried out. If it were it would entirely deprave the Negroes, whose only hope of moral improvement lies in hard work. It may, however, have a considerable effect on the Presidential election. Hitherto, the Negroes have been content not to vote, or to vote, as the Whites direct. It is possible that the hope of a pension may make them break away from the control of the Democrats, and vote the Republican ticket.

The Spectator, 22 August 1891

Why have a pension fund

A pension fund seems to have an immensely complicated structure. It is governed by deeds, booklets and legislation. It has to take account of the needs (sometimes conflicting) of employers, members and trustees. The calculations which need to be undertaken seem to be understandable only by an Einstein. Its advisers and managers have to worry about transfer values, splitting on divorce, and compliance with Pensions Act rules and Inland Revenue rules.

Why bother with all the expense of administration, and with the fees of lawyers, actuaries and accountants? Would it not be simpler for the employer simply to pay the employees a little more money each week that they can use to save for their old age – or just put them on a reduced pay scale after retirement?

That is, in fact, just what used to happen in the nineteenth century – and in practice what happens to civil servants even today. But there are major problems with the simple approach:

- The difficulty with people making their own provision for their own old age is simply that in practice most do not. There are always more pressing needs – housing, food, holidays – and by the time old age becomes a worry, and the urgency to save increases, it is a little late. Just before the turn of the century Charles Booth discovered that the main cause of poverty was simply old age – and that exhorting people to save for their old age was for most people simply impossible. Few employers want their long-serving employees coming back to them in years-to-come looking for financial support.

- The drawback with an employer simply promising to look after an employee in old age is that (unless he is the government) there is no certainty that he will still be there to meet his promise when it falls due. In any event, few employees now work for their entire career with one employer. It is more sensible for funds to be set aside each working year to meet the employer's promise, as a guarantee fund.

- Finally, whatever the administrative costs of most company pension schemes, they are a major bargain compared with the often extreme costs of personal pensions. And they invariably offer immensely better value-for-money.

Many, progressive, employers have established pension schemes using a system which is now the envy of much of the rest of the world. Even the French, who have a very different and much praised system, are now planning to copy the UK arrangements for company pensions.

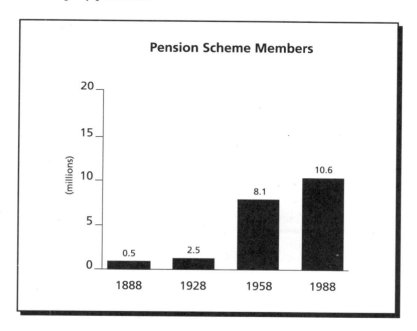

Drawbacks to pension funds

Pension funds are not perfect – and they do not suit everybody:

- a final salary company scheme may not be appropriate, for example, for a young person who expects to stay only a year or two with the company;

- transfer values offered by most schemes, while they are immeasurably superior to those offered only a few years ago, will not necessarily be adequate to buy the corresponding length of service with the new employer;

- sometimes communications are not all they should be;

- sometimes, fortunately very rarely, assets can be fraudulently removed from the scheme, as they can from any other form of savings arrangements, or investment returns may be less than expected; there is however a compensation fund which can operate in such cases;

- compliance with regulatory requirements can be bureaucratic, expensive and time-consuming, but no more nowadays than any other similar area of activity or other forms of pension arrangements.

But for most people, in most circumstances, company pension funds offer better value for money, greater security and greater peace of mind than the alternatives. This applies to the employer as well as the employee.

Why have a trustee?

The relationship between the employer, the employee and the pension fund is a useful one to understand:

- the employer promises to provide not only pay but a pension (often dependent on years of employment and salary levels) in exchange for which the employee promises to work;

- both employer and employee agree to make contributions to the scheme. Even where it is a 'non-contributory scheme', ie the employee makes no actual contributions, the courts consider that the employer's contributions can be seen as the employee's deferred pay.

As a trustee you hold the money on behalf of the employees (and employer) to make sure it is properly looked after. In most cases, it is not your job to interfere with the bargaining between employer and employee; you are merely a guardian of the pot. In exceptional circumstances, such as where an employer seeks a refund of a pension fund surplus, you may have a duty to bargain with the employer to ensure that members get a fair deal.

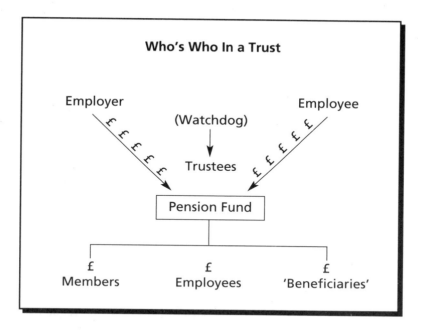

Why have a trust?

Trusts seem odd animals; would it not be simpler – or at least more familiar – to use a company, instead, to run a pension scheme?

There are three reasons why trusts are used:

- *First*, it is essential to put the money which represents the pensions promise made by the employer, *in a separate pot*. In that way, if the employer becomes insolvent, or is unable to fulfil his pensions promise, at least the money is there to meet the promise.

- *Secondly*, a trust is almost tailor made (unlike a company) to cope with the problems of managing money on behalf of other people (the employer and employees). In some cases (especially money-purchase schemes, see below) it is the employees' money, but they may not touch it (for tax reasons) for many years yet.

- *Thirdly*, there are tax benefits by putting contributions in a trust.

Why is trust law so complicated?

Trust law is a special concept, now being copied throughout the developed world. It is special because it recognises that the same property can have two owners at the same time. In the case of pension schemes the legal ownership of the assets of the pension fund is held by the trustees. They can buy and sell the assets, or mortgage them.

But there are other owners – the members of the scheme (and their survivors and dependants), and the employer. They, however, can only touch their money in special circumstances (set down in the trust documents), eg on retirement or death. The law recognises their rights, and enforces them not through the ordinary legal system (which regulates the trustees), but through a special legal system, invented in the Middle Ages, called equity, since it is based less on strict law (contained for example in Acts of Parliament) than on fair play as the judges see it.

There are therefore two owners of the assets in the pension fund:

- the *trustees* who own the assets *legally*, and

- the *members* and other *beneficiaries* (ie people who may benefit), who own the assets *equitably*.

When enforcing the rights of beneficiaries the court applies general principles of fairness, rather than statutory guidelines (ie set down by Act of Parliament). The court therefore plays a crucial role in the development of trust law – which is changing continually to meet changing social circumstances. It also depends significantly on trustees using their discretion to make many decisions.

But with this great advantage of flexibility, comes a problem – the fluidity of ownership can cause as many difficulties as it solves. One, for example, is the continuing debate on deciding who owns the surplus in a pension fund.

Why were trusts invented?

Being a trustee is a legal position. Trustees own property on behalf of someone else, because the real owners cannot be trusted. It's an old custom – it is said (without much evidence) that it started with the Crusades, when knights entrusted their property to men of repute in case they never returned, until their children were old enough to control their inheritance.

This lack of trust was normally because the real owners were too young, too female (married women had few property rights at that time) or too foolish to manage on their own. Managing property on behalf of others expanded when ownership was separated from control for tax purposes. The person who looks after the property is the trustee; the person on whose behalf the property is owned is called the beneficiary. Beneficiaries of course are not only the members of the scheme – they include anyone else who could benefit – survivors ('widows and widowers' is a bit of a mouthful, and this is an equal opportunity book), dependent children and other dependants.

Trust law has a slightly chequered history – it developed mightily in the time of Henry VIII as a device to help avoid tax. The system, however, was found to be useful in many other areas – and today is used to regulate charities, unit trusts and international securities such as Eurobonds. And its principles are applied to many other fields such as the duties of directors in companies.

What is a trust?

A trust is a little like an elephant – most lawyers at least can recognise it when they see it, but defining it has always been a problem.

WHAT IS A TRUST?

A Legal Definition

"An equitable obligation, binding a person (who is called a trustee) to deal with property over which he has control (which is called trust property) for the benefit of persons (who are called the beneficiaries or cestuis que trust) of whom he may himself be one and any one of whom may enforce the obligation."

Underhill & Hayton on Trusts

A simple definition..........

What is a trustee?

A trustee is simply a person who looks after a trust. He can be an individual, a group of individuals or even a company. His job is to ensure the assets of the trust are well looked-after. Over the years the courts have set down the way in which a trustee should work, and has defined:

- some duties

- some discretions

- some liabilities.

All these are discussed later.

You have been appointed as a trustee not to be an expert, but to apply your common sense, experience of the world, and integrity, to the care of other peoples' money.

What kind of trustee am I?

A trustee is usually a person, an individual (normally, there is more than one). Sometimes the trustee is a company, which offers advantages of continuity (you don't need to keep changing the deed everytime someone retires or is appointed) and gives some additional protection against liability.

You might be a trustee of a *self-administered* fund, ie where the investment management and administration is dealt with in-house – or of an *insured* fund, where all that is taken care of by an insurance company.

You might be elected by your colleagues in the workforce – or appointed by the employer. But whatever your origins, and however big your head, you can only wear one hat around the trustees' table – that of trustee. All your other obligations and interests must be set aside in favour of the members of the scheme and the other beneficiaries.

In some cases there is a *corporate trustee,* ie a company which is a trustee. In that case you are a director of the trustee company, rather than a trustee yourself – but you have to behave like a trustee nonetheless. The advantages of being a director of a trustee company include that it is easier to resign, you have added (though not complete) protection from litigation, and there are savings in documentation – sometimes.

There is talk occasionally of *independent trustees.* All trustees are supposed to be independent – you are supposed to represent the interests of the beneficiaries, if necessary at the expense of the interests of the employer, the trade union or any other group you may also represent the interests of. An independent trustee normally means in fact a trustee who does not have a conflict of interest – or, where an employer has become insolvent, a trustee required by law to be in place to help safeguard the interests of members.

Who makes a trust — and how?

Anyone can make a trust. In a pension scheme, normally it is the employer, who signs a document (called a trust deed) which simply declares:

- that a trust shall exist;

- who the trustees are who will look after it;

- how it will get its income (contributions from employer and employees); and

- how it will be administered.

Trust law and other law

Trust law is only one part of the law; other sources of regulation include Acts of Parliament, the discretions of government departments and the trust document itself, not to mention the contracts of employment. The sources that need to be checked when determining a problem are therefore widespread.

The law is normally applied, if necessary by lawyers and if the problem has to go to court, by judges. While many people quite rightly have the view that the law is an ass, and that judges, not to mention solicitors, do not have minds that think like the rest of us, it should also be noted that they are also human. In practice many decisions are made not so much on the basis of the law but in accordance with common sense – although not always.

Jargon

Jargon is one of the drawbacks to pensions – and when coupled with trust law jargon, can make life highly confusing. But in fact in trust law, there are only a few buzz-words, and it helps to sort them out at the beginning:

- *the settlor* – means the person who creates the trust and in a pensions trust is usually the employer;

- *the trust property* – means the assets of the fund;

- *the beneficiaries* – means not only the members, but also their families and dependants, and anyone else who may take a benefit from the trust – including sometimes the employer.

Why is trust law different from other law?

Trust law was invented to cope with the fact that the ordinary law clearly resulted in some injustice; it had become obsolete and oppressive. Trust law was designed to be flexible, to change with the times, and to use general principles of fairness and justice (not just strict rules of law) that would apply to a range of situations.

In time it developed its own arthritic tendencies, but a former regulator, called the Occupational Pensions Board recognised, for example, that the flexibility and equity performed by trust law has some major advantages. Few informed people now suggest that pension funds should be governed by any other structure.

It has its drawbacks though, because since it is based on principles of fairness and equity, it is not always possible to say with certainty what the outcome of any question might be; but the alternative of certainty, theoretically possible under an Act of Parliament, is now much less popular. Acts of Parliament (statutes) can create as many, if not more, problems than they solve. The Financial Services Act in 1986, for example, was designed to protect investments, created what is now the large infrastructure known as the Financial Services Authority with a raft of regulations and regulators – but was unable to prevent a major scandal of the 1990s, the Maxwell Affair. The Pensions Act 1995, also designed to protect pensions failed to prevent still later scandals. Indeed it was later found to create almost as many problems as it was designed to solve – and may also have contributed in part to the structural and funding problems that faced pension schemes at the beginning of the twenty-first century. And the Pensions Act 1995 is now beginning to raise all sorts of questions and uncertainties of its own.

Trust deed and rules

The most important document is the Trust Deed. Usually it is in two parts:

- the deed itself, which is the constitution of the trust, dealing with appointment and removal, investment powers and winding-up the trust; and

- the rules, which set out the benefits, the contributions, the Inland Revenue requirements and the 'contracting-out rules' (see below).

The deed and rules can also be changed from time to time — and how the changes are to be made will also set out be set out in the deed.

The deed is king...

The first duty of a pension fund trustee, in theory, is to read the deed. This can be seriously boring, even with a modern so-called Plain English deed. However it is your duty as a trustee to administer the trusts, and in order to do this you must know what is in it.

In practice, the deed will allow you (and indeed expect you) to appoint *'delegates'*, ie other people to do much of your work on your behalf. These people, including managers and advisers, are appointed to administer the terms of the deed – but there are some jobs that you have to do yourself and cannot delegate.

The trust deed now contains huge quantities of information (much of which is rarely referred to in practice, such as revenue limits and contracting-out rules) and you can safely skip these. In any case, as model rules, ie standards produced by the authorities, come into fashion, the content of the guidelines of the Inland Revenue Savings Pensions and Share Scheme (IRSPSS) Office of the Inland Revenue and the Occupational Pensions Regulatory Authority becomes less important.

WHAT TO CHECK IS IN THE DEED

- **The Delegation Power** - that you as a trustee can give your work to professionals to do

- **The Indemnity Provisions** - that you as a trustee in most cases should be excluded from liability for acting as an honest trustee and that the employer will indemnify you against any costs or liabilities — and if necessary insure them. The problem with indemnities is that if the employer goes into liquidation they are worthless

- **The Trustee's Powers** - where does the balance of power in making decisions lie between you and the employer. Sometimes in practice, trustees have few discretions or powers

- **Power to Resign** - that you have a power to resign, perhaps in writing, to avoid having to apply to the court for the right to resign

- **Effect of Wind-up** - that the rules are clear on what happens if the scheme has to be wound up, and in particular what happens if there are any deficits, and who owns any surpluses

- **The Amendment Clause** - how the scheme can be changed, and whether you have a part to play — and that you do not need to apply to OPRA or the Court to keep the documents up to date

In practice, therefore, reading the entire deed is a counsel of perfection. But there are some clauses of the Deed that you really should look at, and you should acquaint yourself with these points if nothing else (see What To Check is in the Deed above).

The document also describes how trustees are appointed, how the trust is administered, and invested, and of course sets out the benefits and contributions.

Anyone can be a trustee – the employer, a trust company, individuals, and employee representatives; in practice the Occupational Pensions Regulatory Authority (rarely) forbids certain people from becoming trustees.

How many trustees? In pension funds the trust deed does not usually lay down a minimum or maximum number of trustees; in practice there should be at least two and probably not more than half-a-dozen to avoid the decision-taking becoming unwieldy.

... but what about the announcements?

Nowadays the announcements to members about their benefits are also regarded as legal documents – despite any statement in them to the contrary. You need to make sure that the employer is not making pension promises through contracts of employment that may affect the solvency of the fund.

Do I need to be 'authorised'?

You do not usually need the permission of anyone in authority to be a trustee. But there are exceptions to this general principle:

- if you are a trustee of a *'small self-administered scheme'*, one of the trustees must be authorised by the Inland Revenue Savings Pensions and Share Scheme (IRSPSS) Office as a *'pensioneer trustee'*, ie a Revenue-approved trustee

- if you carry out *'day-to-day'* management of investments (ie you give orders to buy and sell stocks and shares or other securities on a day-to-day basis) you need to be authorised under the Financial Services and Markets Act and regulated by the Financial Services Authority.

For most trustees, the hassle and expense of being authorised, and the continual reporting requirements make it not worthwhile, which is why in almost all cases, investment management is delegated to someone who is authorised.

The fact that you are not authorised, however, does not mean that you cannot make decisions on 'strategic' investment matters, eg how much of the fund should be in gilts, or whether you should adopt ethical investment principles (see below, page 46).

You are expected, however, to undertake training (and are entitled to time off with pay for that) and the Occupational Pensions Regulatory Authority can suspend you or prohibit you from trusteeship if you misbehave.

Can I be a trustee?

Almost anyone can be a trustee – you do not need to be qualified, or even experienced. But certain people are not permitted to be a trustee of a pension fund:

- if you have been convicted of a crime involving dishonesty or deception (unless it has been 'spent', ie was many years ago)

- if you have been made bankrupt

- if you are a company with directors who have been convicted of a crime involving dishonesty or deception, or have been made bankrupt

- if you have been disqualified by the court from acting as a company director

- if you are disqualified by the Occupational Pensions Regulatory Authority

If any of these events happens after you have been appointed, you automatically stop being a trustee. If you behave as a trustee while disqualified you could be prosecuted.

Employee trustees

Members of a scheme have a right to nominate up to a third of the trustees. This is normally organised by the employer, but if he does not do so, it is your duty to make arrangements to invite members to make nominations. The details (which are complex) will be organised by your advisers.

Training

Trustees do not need to be qualified. But you are entitled to time off for training if you wish, and you would be vulnerable to criticism if you never take any training. One day's (good) training is usually sufficient (see p.204) although if you wish to expand your education and learn about investments and actuarial techniques, by all means do so.

Your employer must give you 'reasonable' time off work both to perform your duty as trustee and also for training. 'Reasonable' is something of a weasel word, but you need to take account of how much training is needed, how much time is taken off for training generally, the circumstances of the employer's business and how crucial your day-to-day presence is.

You are entitled to pay at normal or average hourly rates while taking time off; if you have a problem you can complain to an industrial tribunal.

Employment protection

One of the major concerns of new trustees is the fear of incurring the wrath of an employer if they take a decision in the interests of the trust but against the interests of the employer.

If this is a concern for you, you should not take the position of trustee in the first place – or should resign. At the same time the employer is not allowed to dismiss you for performing your duties (or proposing to perform your duties); if you are dismissed it is unfair dismissal. Nor can an employer treat you adversely because of the way you act as trustee. Industrial tribunals can, in suitable cases, award not only compensation but also reinstatement.

Duties, discretions and powers

Trustees of pension funds have three jobs; they have to exercise duties, discretions and powers:

- A duty is a specific obligation to do something. One example is to look after the funds.

- A discretion is a power to make a choice. One example is to decide whether to pay a death benefit to a wife or a mistress.

- A power is a right to do something. One example is a power to appoint a fund manager.

Sometimes powers, discretions and duties are mixed up; but there are separate rules applying to each function. The next Chapter looks at just what those rules are.

Statutory obligations

The Pensions Act 1995 imposes a set of additional obligations, with accompanying penalties for breach. A list of these is set out in Appendix IX; in practice most of them will be delegated to advisers to carry out.

It would be sensible to obtain confirmatory letters from your advisers as follows:

- from your solicitor – that the documents comply with the Act, in particular in relation to dispute resolution;

- from your actuary – that the funding position is satisfactory under the Act;

- from your administrator (or, where appropriate, your insurer) – that they are monitoring the receipt of contributions from the employer;

- from your employer (or administrator) – that the member-nominated trustee rules have been complied with.

3

TAKING OFFICE

Sir – In your interesting article on "Old-Age Pension," in the Spectator of July 16th [1898] you suggest that, if practicable, 7s a week for every one would be deliverance out of his present distress. Are you prepared to put Englishmen into leading-strings and dole the pittance out daily? Otherwise privation and misery will again triumph. At our Guardians' Board meeting last week an army pensioner was before us "starving and destitute". He had 7s 7d a week, but it is paid once a quarter in advance. It was paid on July 1st, and on July 14th he appealed for admittance into our workhouse. "What will you do with me, I am starving?" Can any scheme cure drinking and recklessness? I am Sir, &c.

The Spectator, July 1898

Introduction

Some trustees are normally appointed trustee by the employer; others are appointed under a process designed to enable members to nominate trustees.

Whichever way you are appointed, there are a number of initial tasks to complete, and some things to check out. In a perfect world you might have checked some major items before appointment, but in practice things do not work out like that.

The first things to do are:

- inspect the documents (see Chapters 2 & 4), and

- find out when you and the other trustees meet in order to exercise your duties, discretions and powers.

The art of good trusteeship is efficient and competent delegation of most of your functions. This chapter looks at what your functions are, what can be delegated, and what cannot.

You already know that you have certain:

- duties,

- discretions and

- powers

as a trustee.

This chapter sets out what they are, and how best to perform them. In law, there are complex rules laid down as to how you should exercise these duties, discretions and powers. But in practice, common sense should usually suffice, dosed with a little outside advice when perplexed.

Your main problem is avoiding conflicts of interest, or suggestions of conflict. Pension fund trustees are particularly susceptible to that charge, since they may wear several hats at once: trustee, member, employer and even adviser.

Properly documented decisions, proper accounting and actuarial systems, and solid legal support are all essential to avoid falling into obvious traps. The job of pension fund trustees is not, in the normal course of events, to bargain for benefits, but merely to safeguard the assets supporting the promised benefits — a principle which some union trustees in the past have not always found easy to follow.

CHECKLIST ON APPOINTMENT

- Have you seen the trust deed and rules:

  - Does it have an indemnity clause?
  - Does it have an exoneration clause?
  - Does it allow you to retire without going to court?
  - Does it allow you to insure yourself – and allow the scheme to pay the premium?
  - Can it be altered or amended easily?
  - What is the balance of power between the employer and the trustees?

- Do you have a full house of advisers:

  - Actuary?
  - Solicitor?
  - Accountant?
  - Investment Manager?
  - Administrator?

- Is the scheme approved:

  - By the Inland Revenue (inspect the letter)?
  - By the IRNICO (Inland Revenue National Insurance Contributions Office) if contracted-out?

- Are there any outstanding potential legal claims?

- Have you got copies of:

  - The annual trustees report?
  - The last actuarial report?
  - The accounts?
  - The last investment manager's report?
  - Letters from the actuary, lawyer and administrator confirming compliance with the provisions of the Pensions Act 1995

- Is there a training programme for trustees?

- How often do the trustees meet?

  - Where are the previous minutes? What do they say?
  - What is the reporting structure of the pensions manager, investment adviser, pensions consultant and others?

See also the NAPF Checklist for Pension Fund Trustees (appendix vii)

The differences between powers, duties and discretions

It is important to distinguish the *powers, duties* and *discretions*, which you are given when you become a trustee. They can all be found either in the deed or from the general law.

Duties

Duties of trustees include:

- Checking the documents

- Investing the money

- Giving information

- Paying the benefits

- Not making profits out of managing the trust, eg by doing deals with trust property

- Preparing accounts

- To comply with the law, especially the Pensions Act 1995.

A duty is a job which you have to ensure is carried out – though not necessarily by yourself. But they are the basic obligations of the trustee, the obligations which are necessary to ensure that a pension fund is run as a pension fund.

Discretions

Discretions of trustees involve both questions of principle and matters affecting individuals; they could include for example:

- choosing investments (if this has not been delegated)

- deciding who shall get certain benefits on the death of a

member

- deciding whether (subject to the employer's permission) there shall be pension increases

- deciding whether to change the terms of the deed (subject to certain constraints)

- deciding (on advice) whether you should break the terms of the trust

- deciding whether and when to take advice

- deciding when and how to receive transfers into the scheme, and on what terms, and similarly

- deciding when and how and at what level transfers out of the scheme should be paid.

The point of a discretion is simply to allow more flexible management of the trust. There are many decisions that have to be taken that cannot be fully catered for in any document, that need personal knowledge, careful judgment and simple common sense. And there are some problems that simply cannot be foreseen.

These discretions cannot be delegated to anyone else; it is your function as a trustee to take these decisions yourself – using advice if necessary.

Powers

The deed will give you, and the other trustees, certain powers. There may be a power to increase benefits (subject to the approval of the employer). There will always (in a properly drafted deed) be a power to delegate. These powers are not absolute; they must be exercised reasonably – and in the interests of the beneficiaries.

Delegating

In practice many of your duties are delegated: day-to-day investment management (such as choosing which shares to buy) you would normally hand over to an investment manager. And you would not yourself normally check that pensions claims are valid, or personally collect the contributions – although you would expect to be informed if they were not collected. Nor would you, on a daily basis, keep the immensely complicated records that now seem to be needed. But, as mentioned, discretions, for example, cannot be delegated, and in some cases you have to make your own decisions – that is what you are there for.

Even where you have delegated, although you can rely on those you have appointed to carry out your wishes (one of your duties is to examine that they are reputable and competent) it is still your job to supervise them, and to disagree with them if you think they are going wrong or giving wrong advice. You cannot delegate blindly.

Acts of Parliament and other laws

Your primary guide is the trust deed and rules; but they do not

---

STANDARDS OF BEHAVIOUR

When managing the trust: to act with reasonable care and in good faith

When investing the assets: to act as a reasonable prudent man of business when investing other people's money

---

work in isolation, and pension funds are subject to a mountain of law. You do not need to know it intimately, but in brief you may need to know about the following areas:

- **The fiscal law**, being the Inland Revenue constraints on benefits and contributions. The Inland Revenue's approval is crucial to the operation of most schemes, and their rules may limit your actions. Many of the rules are set out in Acts of Parliament (such as Finance Acts); others are set out in Practice Notes, issued by the Revenue (its Savings, Pensions and Share Schemes Office and 'PSO' by 'IRSPSS'), others are contained in occasional memoranda published by the PSO.

- **The social security law**, contained in social security statutes and regulations. These cover, for example:

  - contracting-out
  - preservation
  - transfers
  - equal treatment
  - indexation
  - the Occupational Pensions Regulatory Authority, the Pensions Ombudsman, the Pensions Registry and other organisations
  - what happens on insolvency
  - disclosure of information

  and many other matters.

- **The general trust law**, contained in statutes (Acts of Parliament) and in decisions of the judges made largely over the last 100 years. Whilst valiant attempts have been made by lawyers and others to apply the principles laid down in these cases to the problems of pension funds, most are relevant more to family trusts, and much of this kind of law is dated and not applicable.

- **Other law**, which only indirectly applies to pension fund trustees, such as the Data Protection Act, which will require you to register if the pension records are held on computer (usually) or requires you to be authorised if you give investment advice (under the Financial Services and Markets Act). In almost all cases, this legislation is not a matter for you to worry about – your managers will make sure that you have delegated your functions.

At one time, there was very little statute law to worry trustees. There were the tax statutes and that was about it. Now there are acres of social security rules, contracting-out details, preservation, transfer rules, disclosure regulations, rules about accounting, more rules about mergers and takeovers not to mention the Pensions Ombudsman and the Pensions Registry – and of course the mass of regulations following the Pensions Act 1995. There is also the seemingly impenetrable law about equal treatment for men and women, which involves European law mostly.

No one expects trustees to know all this, even though you must comply with it. What you are expected to do is to listen to advice (not necessarily to take it) and to ensure that others, ie the managers and advisers, comply with it. There are some things that you have to check yourself, such as some details of the company law provisions; but by and large however, sleepless nights can be avoided.

Contents of Statutes 'Statutes', in this Chapter, also includes statutory instruments – regulations the making of which is delegated to one of the government departments. Between them these two forms of laws comprise some of the most difficult and complex ever invented, and the interpretation of which often defeats trained experts. Whether their standard will improve is another matter; but, as ever, much can be overcome by using advice, the trustee's security-blanket.

What to watch out for

There are one or two traps for the unwary in being a trustee. The most common include:

- conflicts of interest

- inadequate trustee protection

- obsolete documentation, especially deeds which contain no power to resign or amend the documentation

Most of these are discussed later in the book; at this stage it is sufficient to be aware of the existence of these traps, and take the necessary safeguards. The checklist should help.

Conflicts of interest

There are particular problems facing trustees, especially:

- those of conflict of interest, where they occupy different positions

- payment, where trustees are professional trustees

You should be careful to check the deed gives you power to be paid (if you are paid) and to get benefits from the scheme despite the fact you are a trustee.

4

THE PAPERWORK

In the little town of Sanary-sur-Mer in the Var lived, so their neighbours thought, two devoted spinster daughters. Although their mother was over 90 and to ill to go out, they both stayed at home to look after her.

This week, however, they found out just how the two sisters were looking after their mother. the discovery followed the attempt by a local town hall official to deliver a letter addressed to the mother, Mme Helene Barbaroux.

No matter how hard he tried he found he could not get past the two daughters, Jeanne and Genevieve, who told him through the barely open door that their mother was too ill to see him and was in fact being treated by the doctor.

The town hall official became suspicious. The doctor they mentioned had been dead to his certain knowledge for the past six years. he went to the police who obtained a warrant and went to call on Mme Barbaroux.

The two sisters would not let the police in. Eventually they called the fire brigade and the door was forced open.

Inside they found Mme Barbaroux wrapped in a coat. She had been dead for the past three or four years. It was impossible to tell exactly how long.

For all that time the sisters had kept their mother's death a secret and used to move her about the house wrapped in the coat whenever it was necessary to hide her from a visitor. The elder sister, aged 63, usually slept with her mother's body on the bed beside her.

By keeping the death a secret the two sisters were able to continue to draw their mother's pension, which although small, made a great difference to their meagre incomes.

The Times, 14 August 1980

Introduction

Pension funds seem to breed paper, and if you are not a paper person, the quantity and length of documentation can be a little overwhelming. Documents can prove difficult to understand; many of them are very long; many of them are written in 'pension-ese'.

It is not sensible to attempt to read them all word-for-word. But there are things you should look for when you first become a trustee.

For example, there should be power in the deed to take independent advice on the implications of the deed. If the deed is not satisfactory or exposes you too greatly to risks which you are not prepared to take, either have the document changed, or refuse to act as trustee. Most deeds can be changed, even to reduce benefits, and most documents need continual revision to bring them into line with current law and practice.

The deed

The deed is in a way the constitution of the scheme. Even Plain English deeds can be very long, and that is not unreasonable. They have to cope with foreseeing many possibilities, some of which may never happen. While the lawyers often say you have to familiarise yourself with the deed (and other documents) this is in modern terms not a sensible or practical requirement. It was in the days when there were short family trusts. Nowadays pension deeds are technical documents; but while no-one really expects you to read them, you should know what is in them – and if necessary where to look something up if you have a problem.

So while it may prove to be a waste of time to read the document, you should make sure that there is an index or a list of contents, and get a feel of what is in it. It will contain the usual terms:

- How the trust is formed

- How it is changed

- How the trustees are appointed and removed – and who they should be

- How the trust is wound up.

The rules

The rules are normally in a separate section of the deed and contain information about the pension scheme itself, such as:

- who can join

- what contributions there are and who pays them

- what the benefits should be

- what happens if the scheme is wound up.

The booklet

The booklet, (which includes 'announcements', 'notices' and any other similar communications about the scheme), must, under Inland Revenue rules, be given to members of the scheme. There are guidelines set down in the Disclosure Regulations as to what should be in them – but not how they should be expressed. With PC's and desktop publishing around these days there is little excuse for them not being in English or set out so that readers with modest ability can understand them.

The employer, of course, sees the scheme less of a benefit than an expense. He will therefore spend at least a little time and money explaining the advantages of an in-house scheme to the employees. The cost of communication is much less than the cost of an unhappy, worried or insecure workforce – which is what it may become if the pensions are inadequate or, more importantly, *perceived* to be inadequate.

The actuarial valuation

The actuarial valuation, usually at least every three years, gives a picture of how the scheme is doing. It will tell you if the scheme is in surplus or deficit – though it won't tell you what those terms mean. There is no cause for celebration for a surplus – equally there will not necessarily be a cause for gloom if there is a deficit.

All depends on the assumptions used by the actuary in doing his calculations. What you are looking for is a simple explanation of any problems of the fund as the actuary sees it.

The accounts

The accounts of a pension fund are very simple; money in and money out. The only reason for them is to tell you how much the administration has cost – and whether there has been any theft from or mismanagement of the scheme. The accounts will only give a picture of the fund as at their date; they do not in themselves ensure that the funds are secure, or that problems do not arise after their completion.

The trustees report

This is a report which you have to prepare each year for the use of the members and others, setting out very simply who the managers are, who are the advisers and how they can get in touch with you. It is normally prepared by your advisers.

The statement of investment principles

The statement of investment principles is a relatively new requirement; it must state the objectives of investment. These can include balancing the investments to take care of the different interest groups (for example, pensioners will normally need to have the money representing their interests in, say, bonds; active members (employees) will be better protected by investments in shares. The reason is that active members can live with fluctuating values in shares; pensioners will be happier with more stable investment even though the returns may be lower). It will normally be prepared by the advisers, after you have considered written advice from them, but the employer must be consulted before it is approved by you.

The investment managers report

Investment managers' reports for even modest pension funds are these days, thanks to the computer, of a size which requires the devastation of a small Amazonian forest. And it is often difficult to see the wood for the trees. You are really looking for comparative performance against the market – has your fund done as well as others in the marketplace. If not ask him why not. The other thing to check is whether the investments match the rules of the scheme – and whether there is sufficient diversification.

Advisers' contracts

All advisers must now provide you with a contract, setting out their obligations to you as trustee. This is to ensure they are aware that if they also act for the employer, their prime duty is to you.

Inland Revenue undertakings

The Inland Revenue usually requires the trustees to sign certain promises – for example to tell them when changes have been made to the documents, or discuss with them if benefits are to be changed significantly.

You may have to re-sign these undertakings – or take them on board from former trustees. In practice, your advisers will carry out most of the undertakings.

Drafting in English

It is becoming very fashionable for lawyers and others to suggest you might like documents drafted in Plain English. The aim is a very proper one; but in practice the documents that emerge can cause more problems than they solve. There is no excuse nowadays for documents to have arcane English such as 'heretofore', or 'the said', or the innumerable tautologies like 'it is hereby agreed and understood'. If they are in your deed ask your lawyer to take them out; or ask the insurance company to redraft it. You do not have to accept substandard documents from either of them.

But there is a place for jargon. For example, in a car manual, it would be difficult to find a replacement for the word carburettor or manifold, and most car drivers would be hard pushed to recognise one or the other when they saw it. But they still know how to drive the car – and are responsible for it.

Professor Goode, who examined the reform of pensions law after the Maxwell Affair, recommended that pension scheme deeds should be rewritten at least every five years. That's probably not a bad idea: the documents should be as short as possible, as simple as possible and as readable as possible; but that is not to say they should or could be as readable as Frederick Forsyth or as simple as Jeffrey Archer. Pensions are not like that.

THE PAPER CHECKLIST

Is there, somewhere, the following:

- The trust deed and rules – and is it updated to take account of the Pensions Act 1995
- A member's booklet, updated to take account of the Pensions Act 1995
- A customer agreement with the investment manager
- A service agreement/letter with the lawyer
- A service agreement/letter with the accountant
- A service agreement/letter with the actuary
- A service agreement/letter with the insurance company
- A letter of advice from an investment adviser (which might be the actuary) on investment policy
- A statement of investment principles
- A set of pension scheme accounts, completed within 7 months of the scheme's year end
- A trustees' report, not more than a year old
- An actuarial report not more than three years old
- An investment manager's report (usually not more than 6 months old)
- A set of Inland Revenue undertakings

5

INVESTING THE ASSETS

Once the Prudential Corporation was the epitome of everything good in English business: patience, sobriety, responsibility and, of course, prudence. Times have changed. The company has just lost £300 million on a catastrophically timed foray into the estate agency business, which cannot be covered even by its charging 14.6 per cent on many of its home loans. So the Pru for the first time in half a century has cut its reversionary bonuses to pensioners, by 8 per cent. But its chief executive, Mr Mick Newmarch, almost simultaneously has been awarded a pay increase of 43 per cent, or £3,000 a week, from £380,190 to £543,673 a year. Mr Newmarch is not a man with a nose for irony. He writes in the Prudential's annual report for the financial year just ended: *'1990 had been a difficult year. For me, it was also a rewarding one.......'*

The organisations who should become active in the matter of top people's pay in the private sector are the big institutional shareholders: it is after all their money that is being spent, or to be more precise, the money of the pensioners and future pensioners they represent. In America, this has started to happen. Recently one fund worth $60 billion voted against the re-election of directors at the multi-national company ITT, because the pay of ITT's chairman had risen 63 per cent, even as the company's profits had stagnated.

No such protest has yet occurred on this side of the Atlantic. If it did of course, the action would have to come from the biggest shareholder of all, the large insurance companies – such as Norwich Union and the Prudential. But, somehow, it is hard to imagine Mr Bridgewater of Norwich Union or Mr Newmarch of the Pru doing any such thing. Humanity can stand only so much irony.

The Spectator, The Limits of Prudence, 18 May 1991

Introduction

One of your major obligations is, not surprisingly, to ensure proper investment of the funds. Good performance can make an astonishing difference either to the contributions that have to be made, or the benefits that can be given. A one per cent difference in the return can make a 25% difference in benefits, for example.

You must (or ensure your managers do):

- comply with the statement of investment principles, required to be produced under the Pensions Act 1995;

- diversify;

- choose appropriate investments, ie appropriate for your needs;

- follow the terms of the deed (which will usually override the Trustee Act 1925 which otherwise tells you how to invest the money);

- appoint investment managers (otherwise be subject to the Financial Services and Markets Act);

- make money for the beneficiaries;

- *invest* the money, rather than speculate with it, or leave it in the bank, or use it for purposes other than the provision of retirement benefits;

- determine investment strategy, rather than specific investments;

- apply the 'prudent man' rule.

Social and ethical investments

You can sometimes adopt social or ethical criteria when deciding investment policy – but trustees have to beware of becoming involved with non-trust objectives. The fund is set up to provide retirement benefits, not to pursue economic, political or ethical objectives. In the famous *Scargill* case the coal miner's leader suggested that the Mineworkers' pension fund should not be used to invest overseas (in the States) or in competing energy industries (such as oil). The court decided that pension scheme money should not be invested in line with the economic policy of the union, but to make as much as possible for the members.

You could still decide not to invest in Iraq or Zimbabwe (say) because of investment worries (civil turmoil, affecting investment returns) or in defence industries (because of the end of the Cold War). And you might think that green investments (industries cleaning up the environment) would be a good investment bet for the future.

Choosing and controlling the investment manager

One major problem is choosing, and then controlling, the investment manager. This could be the insurance company, or a specialist investment manager, or a merchant bank.

They all seem to offer:

• spectacular returns;

• impressive security; and

• splendid lunches.

The first two are items which you as trustee must take seriously: security and return are the basic criteria. Pension funds should adopt lower risk investments than you might personally be prepared to take, and the returns might therefore not be quite so high.

It is your job to ensure that the investment manager is doing his job - complying with the terms of the deed, your investment strategy, and producing returns competitive with the market.

But you can still enjoy the lunches.

Authorisation

If you get too involved with day-to-day investment decisions, you may need to be authorised (see p.22).

Pension fund trustees are not expected to be investment wizards – there are plenty around to choose from. But you do have to:

- monitor the investments,

- see that they have been properly invested by others in accordance with the deed,

- that they have not disappeared,

- see that they have performed at least adequately. In many cases, outstanding performance might cause you to raise an eyebrow, since often good performance may be as a consequence of taking a few risks. While risks might be acceptable in a young pension fund, where you have a mature fund, ie with a lot of pensioners and relatively few contributors, you should be looking for a low risk strategy,

- ensure that it follows the strategy you have laid down,

- trust and like your investment advisers.

In-house investment management

In many larger pension funds it is customary for the funds to be managed by staff employed by the fund or the employer. It can often result in substantial savings, and in some cases the department can itself be a profit centre rather than a cost.

It will also have to be authorised, of course, and you can be confident that the regulatory supervision is adequate. Nonetheless, as the Maxwell Affair demonstrated, things can go wrong, and the degree of supervision needed is slightly higher.

'Low risk and high risk strategies', 'ethical investment strategies', and 'beauty parades' are terms you need to become familiar with – but if you never know the difference between longs and shorts, or get a bit muddled about just what a derivative is, do not worry. Your advisers should explain to you – and if they do not or cannot, ask again or change your adviser. A useful rule of thumb is to refuse to invest in anything you do not understand.

Monitoring

You should also decide whether you know whether your fund is performing well or poorly. Investment monitoring services can help with this for larger funds; smaller funds are often at the mercy of an insurer who will blind you with science. Outside advice might be helpful.

Poor results over the last few years may mean it is time to change investment manager or insurance company. On the other hand, it may be just the wrong time to change – one fund in the United States changes its fund managers each year to the worst performing fund manager the year before on the assumption he could not do worse this year.

The 'Customer Agreement'

By law your investment manager has to sign an agreement which sets out the terms under which he manages the fund's assets. The law was designed to protect the trustees of pension funds and others; however most such contracts protect the investment manager from almost everything short of nuclear war. These agreements should always be vetted by your lawyers; points to look out for are:

- soft commission deals, where your manager can use stockbrokers who charge high dealing fees, but provide kickbacks to the manager. Perfectly legal if disclosed, but not a proper way to do business;

- whether he has power to engage in 'funnies', such as futures, options and swaps (often called 'derivatives'). Unless you are a trustee of a highly sophisticated fund, it is most unlikely you should want to do this;

- whether he can engage in 'stock-lending', that is use the shares of the fund to lend to other investment people for a fee. There is nothing wrong with it, but you should be aware of the risks involved;

- whether he has read your deed, which may contain special investment rules.

Corporate governance

Trustees nowadays are being encouraged to be involved in the companies they invest in. There is a balance between being an 'absentee landlord' (and letting companies do what they want, your only sanction being to sell their shares if you are unhappy) and interfering on a daily basis (which you have neither the time nor inclination to do – and anyway you are not there to run other people's companies).

There are occasions, such as where there are huge increases in the chief executive's pay, or there is some hanky-panky alleged in the press, where you should use the votes that shareholders have (usually called 'proxies'). How you use those votes should be agreed beforehand with the investment manager; in most cases you will not need to bother.

Self-investment and loanbacks

Sometimes your employer might suggest it would be a good idea for your fund to either lend the company some money, buy one of its factories, buy a few company shares to 'show willing', or engage in a joint venture.

Until recently, you might have had a difficult job fending off such a request – and anyway in many cases the suggestions were good ones. Now, however, such 'self-investment' is strictly controlled, and you should take expert legal advice.

Fashion: risk and reward

You may feel, as you are dealing with what used to be 'widows and orphans' funds, that you should be very cautious in the nature of investments and the choice of manager.

But avoiding risk has a cost. Thirty years ago pension funds restricted their investments to government bonds and mortgages. But while safe, the returns meant that contributions had to be much higher. So, over the years, pension funds have moved progressively into stocks and shares (the Fifties), property (the Sixties), overseas assets (the Seventies) and venture capital (the Eighties). Some feel that the Nineties will see a move into derivatives. Each change of investment policy has involved accepting a higher degree of risk. In almost all cases the risk has paid off – but there are prices to pay, as the Maxwell Affair in 1991 demonstrated.

You could avoid 'a Maxwell' arising in your fund. But you would have to remove all discretion from your fund managers, invest solely in government securities, and devote (in the case of a larger scheme) very much more time to supervision. There would be no guarantee that all risk had been removed – and you would probably have diminished the return to the fund, for which your members will not thank you. As in all these matters, you are expected to make a balanced judgment between risk and reward – and sometimes, fortunately very rarely, it will go wrong.

Tax

One of the major advantages of a pension fund is that it does not pay tax on its investment income – unless:

- there is a surplus (as defined by the Revenue, not your actuary) which is not otherwise dealt with, or

- you do something which the trust shouldn't do, such as pay benefits over the Revenue limits, or

- you do something which is not an investment, ie something which is regarded by the Revenue as 'trading'. In practice that is not your problem, but that of the investment manager.

One of your duties is to ensure that nothing is done to prejudice the tax status of the fund.

6

PROVIDING INFORMATION

A Guardian survey (22 October) reveals that state pensions in Britain are one-third of those in Germany. And one of those British legal quirks which give such charm to our lives lets companies raid the employees' pension fund when they need a bit more cash to buy this year's Porches for the directors. Yes, the KGB in Russia is worse than the British government in Britain. But what damage has the KGB ever done in Britain compared to that done by the British Authorities? Rather it was the spectre of Communism which made our rulers pretend to be a bit civilized and, now that it is dead, we will soon lament the good old days when our pensions were as much as a third of Germany's.

George Stern, Incompetent Buffoons, review of Inside the KGB:
Myth and Reality by Vladimir Kuzichkin, in Literary Review,
December 1990

Introduction

Trustees have always had to provide information to beneficiaries – and pension fund trustees are no exception.

For several years there have been special rules for pension fund trustees (in addition to the general trust law) and these are known in the industry as **'disclosure regulations'**. The information must be made available to a wide range of people – not only the members – including spouses, dependants and others (including sometimes trade unions) who are entitled to a range of information.

Some of the information must be provided automatically; some of it must be provided on request.

WHAT MEMBERS ARE ENTITLED TO AUTOMATICALLY

- New members, scheme details within 13 weeks of joining scheme
- Leavers, rights and options as soon as possible
- Beneficiaries, any change of address for enquiries within 1 month
- Members, (in money purchase scheme) annual benefit statements
- Everyone, changes in scheme details
- Everyone, if winding-up begins

WHAT MEMBERS ARE ENTITLED TO ON REQUEST

- refunds available
- transfers and leaving service rights, no more than once a year
- a copy of the deed and rules, on payment of a reasonable fee
- a copy of the actuarial valuation, on payment of a reasonable fee
- benefit statements, no more than once a year
- scheme details (non members) no more than every three years
- trustees annual report

WHO IS ENTITLED TO INFORMATION?

- Members
- Dependants
- Spouses
- Trade Unions

Whether there is a claim under the regulations or the general law, it is prudent to ensure that members do not receive trustees' minutes, which may relate to personal matters affecting an individual. In principle, however, members are entitled to a copy of the trustees' deliberations – so it is as well to make them fairly broad – you do not want members complaining that your decisions were unreasonable or failed to take certain information into account. Drafting minutes, especially trustee minutes, is a skilled task, and should be delegated to an experienced scriptwriter.

Failure to comply

If you fail to comply with the regulations, there are the usual penalties specified (see Appendix IX). Furthermore, anyone who is aggrieved can complain to the Pensions Ombudsman, or to the County Court. So far as is known, no trustee has yet been convicted of a failure to supply information under the regulations, and even if you do fail for some reason or another, a good excuse, such as the managers or administrators have let you down, will probably suffice. The main answer is to find a good administrator.

Policy

There should be no reason why anyone should not have any information, provided they do not ask too often, or are prepared to pay copying charges where a large volume is in demand. The only time you need to refuse to assist is where personal confidential information is sought, or where a trustee's discretion is questioned, in which case hunt for the nearest lawyer.

Communication

There is no law that says that the way in which you inform your members and others should be clear, simple and helpful. But good communication can often be the valve that lets out the steam from people's ears, and reduces the pressure on you. A little bit of communication goes a long way, and there are now many organisations that specialise in pensions communication.

7

PAYING BENEFITS

'Why Elsie! You must be a rich woman,' said Mr Earlforward. 'What with your wages and your pension!' He spoke without looking at her, in a rather dreamy tone, but certainly interested.

'Well sir,' Elsie replied, 'it's like this. I give my pension to my mother. She's a widow, same as me, and she can't fend for herself.'

'All of it? Your mother?'

'Yes sir.'

'How much is your pension?'

Twenty-eight shillings and eleven pence a week sir.'

'Well, well.' Mr Earlforward said no more. He had often thought about her war pension, but never about any possible mother or other relative. He had never heard mention of her mother. He thought how odd it was that for years she had been giving away a whole pension and nobody knew about it in Riceyman Steps.

Arnold Bennett, Riceyman Steps, 1923

Eligibility

Who can join the scheme is set down in the deed, and is usually a matter only for the employer to decide. You should not let anyone in who is not eligible; you should not exclude those who can join.

But there are grey areas. Suppose your fund has a surplus, but the employer wants a whole new factory full of employees to join, and pay in a miserable transfer value. Do you have to accept them? It will depend on the deed.

But you should be aware that you should not discriminate on the grounds of sex or colour – although you can still discriminate on the grounds of age.

Death benefits

Death benefits are not strictly a pension, but a 'retirement benefit' akin to an insurance benefit. How you pay and to whom you pay is often at your discretion (see below).

Winding-up

Winding-up a scheme can be a traumatic event. It can happen if the employer goes bust, or decides for other reasons to close the scheme. If that happens special rules fall into play which allocate how the benefits are to be split up; if there is not enough money in the fund, benefits may have to be reduced all round. If there is too much you may be able to enhance them.

Divorce

Members who become divorced may have their benefits subjected to a court order that requires some or all of any benefits to be paid to their former spouse – when they fall due. The trustees must comply with the court order, so the records need to be noted. Any order in relation to pensions comes to an end once either party has died or the former spouse has remarried. Any lump sum order however survives death or remarriage. The court also now has the power to divide pension rights at divorce and award the spouse a transfer value as decided by the court.

Members and other beneficiaries

When making decisions, you should take all the beneficiaries into account – not just current employees. Beneficiaries include the spouses and dependents of members, former members (deferred pensioners – which may include people who have left the company) and in some cases the company itself, since if there is a surplus it might in some cases expect to have an interest in the return of some of the surplus. In any case in most instances it will have an interest in keeping contributions down – and returns on the investments high.

It is the job of a trustee not to discriminate between any of the groups of members and other beneficiaries. This does not mean that you have to split any extra funds equally between them – you can decide in certain cases that one group is more deserving of attention that others – but you must consider them all.

Discretions

Exercising discretions is one of the great bugbears of trustees; many of them hate it, and try to obtain clearance from all sorts of other people before doing so.

This is a mistake. One of the reasons you are a trustee is because some people think you are a reasonable kind of a person well able to make common sense judgments. You don't have to get the judgments right; by definition many such decisions will with hindsight be wrong. But provided on balance you get more decisions right than wrong, you will be loved by your members.

Neither can anyone criticise your decisions, provided they are made honestly, reasonably and when in possession of sufficient information – and the court and the Pensions Ombudsman will be very reluctant indeed to interfere with your decisions unless they are clearly crazy – in which case you will have no objection to being overruled.

The kinds of problems in which your discretion is needed are relatively few:

- Choosing advisers – a problem which has already been discussed;

- Deciding who gets the 'death-in-service' benefit. If one of your members dies whilst working,it is likely that his life is insured for anything up to four times his salary. In order to avoid inheritance tax on that money, you have been given the discretion as to whom that money can go to. Normally the dead member will have left a letter saying who he wants it to go to – but sometimes other people come out of the woodwork, such as an undiscovered mistress, or hidden children – who feel they have a claim.

What you do is up to you and your colleagues, although you must ensure that the beneficiary you choose is within the class of people defined in the rules. Take as much information as you can get, if necessary take some advice – but the buck stops with you, and you can either decide to follow the instructions of the dead member, or split it in some other way. The only guardian is your conscience.

- Deciding how to split the investment portfolio between say a series of investment managers

- Deciding to give a pension to a dependant, and deciding whether someone is truly dependant

- Deciding whether someone is ill enough to enjoy an ill-health pension.

Many of these decisions are hard, and will affect the financial security and well-being of someone you may know quite well. Some of the decisions you make may be uncomfortable and difficult ones. But that is what you are there for.

The purpose of discretionary benefits. Using discretions in paying benefits needs a brief understanding of why you have been given those discretions. You may already know that you are given a discretion as to whom to pay any death-in-service benefit to. Most schemes contain this benefit, which provides a substantial sum in cash if the member dies while working. To avoid it falling into the estate of the dead member (and thereby possibly subject to inheritance tax) the trustees can decide who to pay it to. This makes the payment tax-free. But in practice the member will have filled in a 'nomination letter' telling you who he would like the money to go to. The big question is – do you follow the letter? For example, if there is £100,000 to dispose of, and the letter tells you to pay the money to his girl friend, but you know that there is a wife and six grieving children to support, what do you do? Follow the dead man's wishes? Or follow your own conscience? Some trustees take the view that the reason for their having the discretion is only to avoid the tax; others take the view that if they have the discretion they should exercise it. There is no 'proper' answer. However, according to a decision of the Pensions Ombudsman, if you find yourself sleeping with the deceased member's surviving partner, you should abstain from the decision-making.

8

TAKING ADVICE

> Initially, Hoffa had employed hoods much as employers had done. Bosses hired the Mob to break strikes. Hoffa used goons to beat strike-breakers and to bomb and burn the property of recalcitrant employers.
>
> The price he paid was high. Mobsters were allowed to take control of a number of union locals which were used to run protection rackets. The pickings became far richer when multi-billion dollar pension funds were established in the Fifties. The payments came from employers but the funds were controlled by the union. The Mob insisted that investments were made in mafia-controlled businesses.
>
> Yet analysis indicates that Teamster funds out-performed similar funds run on more orthodox lines by other unions.
>
> *John Torode, The dirty workhorse dumped by the Mob,*
> *The Independent, 15 October 1991*

Introduction

As mentioned, trustees are not supposed to know everything themselves – or even very much. They are supposed however to take advice, although they are not required (indeed they must not) follow it if they are unhappy with it. But they must use their advisers to the full, especially their legal advisers, if they are to avoid suggestions that they acted improperly in coming to their various decisions. With the increasing tendency to litigation, following similar trends in the United States, trustees now need protection more than ever – and advice is one of the best protections.

There is a wide range of advisers involved in pensions matters, not all of whom will be appropriate to your scheme, and some of whom will provide more than one element of advice. In principle, most schemes will need one or more of the following:

- Lawyers

- Actuaries

- Accountants

- Pensions consultants

- Pensions managers

- Investment managers

Many advisers are in practice chosen not by you, but by the employer. There is nothing wrong with this – and in many cases the advisers will already be advising the company on other matters and therefore be aware of the particular nature of the business.

But increasingly nowadays there are 'conflicts of interest'; that is, the interests of the members may not be adequately represented by advisers who have a separate duty and loyalty to the employer. The law requires you to ensure they have written to you setting out what they think their obligations are.

As a trustee therefore you will need sometimes to engage advisers for the scheme – either where no such adviser is in place, or where existing advisers find themselves unable to continue to act. And you will need to review continually your relationship with all the advisers.

Lawyers

Choosing a good pensions lawyer can add ten years to your lifespan. The relief is immense. How to choose one is not easy. A list of pensions lawyers is printed in the back of *Pension Funds and Their Advisers*, and on a good day the Association of Pensions Lawyers may let you have its membership list. But all those do is give you a list – not tell you who is good – or, more importantly, good for you, because lawyers are like cheeses – there are lots of good ones, but not everybody likes the taste of some or can afford the best of others.

TEN QUESTIONS TO ASK YOUR LAWYER

- Does he specialise in pensions work, or is it a sideline?
- How many pension schemes of your nature does he act for?
- Can he cope both with drafting documents – and being involved in merger negotiations?
- How does he charge, and how much?
- If there is something to complain about, who is in charge?
- What is his view on Plain English drafting?
- How does he keep up to date with legal developments?
- Does he respond to queries, or play a pro-active role in advising?
- Who does he think he is acting for: the trustees or the employer?
- To whom does he think surpluses belong?

The only answer is to meet a few, invite them to present to you, explain what they do and how they do it – and insist on meeting the person who is going to do the work, not just the senior partner. You may not need a high powered expensive partner for much of your work – on the other hand you need to know that there is an experienced partner available to handle the tricky problems if they arise.

Actuaries

There are two kinds of actuary. *Consulting actuaries* should be on your side, looking at the problems from your point of view (or that of the employer). *Insurance company actuaries* are a very different breed entirely – and mostly have the interests of their employers (the insurance companies) at heart. Remember whose side the actuary is on and half the battle is won.

TEN QUESTIONS TO ASK YOUR ACTUARY

- What is his view on normal actuarial assumptions?
- Is he a consulting actuary or not?
- How does he charge?
- What experience does he have of your kind of fund?
- What kind of report does he produce? Actuarial or English?
- Will he advise you – or the insurer?
- Is he planning to run a surplus – or a deficit?
- How will he handle the data – himself or through a bureau?
- Will he prepare the trustees' report?
- How will he deal with the accountants on FRS 17?

Secondly, can your actuary speak English? Most nowadays are very good, and can speak to ordinary mortals in something approximating to the vernacular. (A lawyer who speaks English is an added bonus, but don't expect too much).

Pension fund managers

Pension fund managers should be distinguished from investment managers. Pension fund managers look after the day-to-day administration of the fund. In the old days it was a job for old Jimmy who was too imbecilic to do anything else. Nowadays it is a highly skilled and technical job, needing knowledge of computer systems, law, administration, finance and some basic actuarial principles.

TEN QUESTIONS TO ASK YOUR PENSIONS MANAGER

- Is he a Fellow or Associate of the Pensions Management Institute?
- Is he computerising your administration – or buying in a package – or keeping it manual?
- Will he arrange for the production of annual reports, benefit statements, accounts – and if he will not, who will?
- Is he responsible for trustee training?
- Is he authorised to manage investments?
- Has he laid-off the insurance obligations – and with whom?
- How many staff will he need?
- Who does he feel his responsibility is to – the employer or the trustees?
- How does he keep up to date?
- What future developments is he anticipating with the fund?

You should be aware of the special problems that pension scheme managers are faced with. Most scheme managers are employed by the employer, and may have a career with the employer. At the same time they have to comply with the trustees' instructions. For most of the time this dual role poses no problem. But there are occasions when the pension scheme manager is placed in an impossible position, with a conflict of loyalty between his employer and his duty to the trustees. You need to be aware of, and sympathetic to, his difficulties, and be prepared to help him – perhaps by taking outside advice.

Some are now qualified as Fellows or Associates of the Pensions Management Institute.

Investment managers

Male investment managers are usually beautifully dressed, with shirts and ties from a secret source in the City not available to ordinary people. Some trustees judge between managers on the cut of their suit – which is not the most sensible criterion. Women investment managers are particularly adept at power-dressing.

TEN QUESTIONS TO ASK YOUR INVESTMENT MANAGER

- How much do they manage?
- How long have they been in business?
- What is their top decile record over the last ten years? And who runs their measurement service?
- Is the man on the beauty parade actually going to manage your money?
- Can you see a sample of their quarterly reports – do you understand it? And, is their customer agreement in plain English?
- Do they take soft commission?
- What are their charges?
- Do they use in-house unit trusts – and is there an additional charge?
- What do they think will happen to the stock market over the next year – and why are they no more in cash?
- What is their strategy?

You need to ensure:

- that they are properly authorised by their relevant body (Investment Managers Regulatory Organisation) and you can check that by ringing up the supervisory body. The larger managers will probably be all right, but some of the smaller managers forget from time to time, and you can be putting your funds at risk;

- that the customer agreement that they propose is a fair one;

- that they have some form of 'fidelity-bond' or insurance against fraud or mismanagement.

You should remember, if you are offered a special, unrepeatable deal with a spectacular return, the history of Barlow Clowes, BCCI and many other newspaper stories.

You should enquire whether the manager is part of an investment monitoring service, so that you can judge how they are doing in comparison with other investment managers.

Pensions consultants

Pensions consultants covers a wide variety of advisers from the specialist pensions consultants with thousands of employees, to the one-man band working from home. The key to a good consultant is not necessarily his size, but his expertise. Checking expertise is extremely difficult; sometimes the only way to judge is either to jump in and try him – or to ask around for experience of his track-record from some other trustees.

A major problem is that many of them work on a commission-based system, rather than a fee-based system – in which case you need to check whether the advice is prompted by commission. At the same time some of the largest advisers, which charge by fees rather than commission, can be let down by their administrative systems.

Accountants

Accountants for pension schemes do not need to be specially skilled – pension fund accounts are some of the simplest to prepare. All they really need to record is money out and in, and whether the investments actually exist. The only problem for a trustee is whether the accountant has a conflict of interests with the employer – for example, if contributions have not been paid by the employer, will the accountant report it immediately to the trustees, or leave it to the following year when the accounts are formally prepared.

It is increasingly common practice to have separate accountants for the pension fund.

Whistle-blowing

Actuaries and accountants must (and other advisers, except solicitors, may) 'whistle-blow', in other words tell the Occupational Pensions Regulatory Authority if they discover something amiss. In theory they must only tell on you if they see something important has gone wrong, but in practice they will send a letter immediately even if the infraction is a minor one. Do not feel aggrieved at this; they have no choice. Be comforted by the fact that the history of whistle-blowing indicates that the first people to suffer from this activity is the whistle-blower, rather than the whistle-blown.

Conflicts of interest

In many cases the same lawyer, actuary, or accountant can act for both you as trustee and the employer. This can save costs and shorten lines of communication.

But there are cases where there are conflicts of interest – in which case your adviser should immediately suggest separate advisers on both sides.

The advice need not thereafter be conflicting or contentious – but it will be independent, and perceived to be independent. The practice of using separate offices of the same adviser, or separate partners in the same firm, is not to be recommended.

9

TRUSTEES AND EMPLOYERS

Prostitutes who have been infected with the Aids virus should be given a pension by the government so they no longer need to work, a leading British doctor says. Such a scheme, already instituted in Vienna, could help to prevent the spread of Aids.

The idea has been suggested by Dr Frank Hull, senior lecturer in general practice at Birmingham University, who said "Maybe the idea will stick in many a moral craw but it makes medical, and ultimately financial, sense."

The plan would decrease the spread of Aids by prostitutes and so reduce the numbers of men and women who contract the disease and eventually require expensive treatment. Aids patients will increasingly compete with other patients for expensive drugs and hospital treatment in the National Health Service.

Dr Hull's idea came from meeting a Viennese doctor....

"Prostitutes in Vienna have been inspected for at least 150 years," Dr Kopp said. "But in June 1985 we started to test them for Aids. So far we have examined 150 women and found eight who are positive. We told the women about our findings and that we could not renew their licence because Aids cannot be cured. We gave them the possibility of a pension from the social welfare fund so that they would not be involved in illegal prostitution." The women were all offered a pension of about 5,000 schillings (about £250) a month.

Oliver Gillie, The Independent, 11 January 1988

Introduction

The employer usually feels that the pension fund is his baby. After all, he has established it, and in most cases he will have paid for it. At the same time, the employees and members (and their unions) have a different approach. It is they who have worked for it, foregone pay increases to ensure contributions are made to it, and have the greater expectations from it. Meanwhile the trustees are watched by both elements: the members are determined that it shall perform up to scratch to provide their benefits; and the employer is concerned that it performs well so as to reduce his contributions in the future.

The balance of power

So it is not surprising that there are sometimes different interests involved in running the scheme. Accordingly, the deed – and the law – sets down who shall be in charge of certain decisions. For example the trustee may have the freedom to improve certain benefits, but subject to the approval of the employer, since it is he who will have to pay for any such improvement.

Since some decisions are made by the employer 'with the consent of the trustees' and some decisions are made by the trustees 'with the consent of the employer', the deed contains certain 'balance of powers'.

These balance of powers come into play especially where surpluses are concerned, and it is reasonable for example for the employer to reserve certain powers for his approval to contain costs. But a series of recent cases has decided that where an employer uses his power in this way he must do so, not necessarily in the best interests of the members, but at least in a fair and reasonable manner. Proving what is fair and reasonable is of course a very different matter.

The legal relationship

The usual arrangement is that the employer and employee make a pensions promise between them (a contract) and the trustees hold the funds as independent security. The trustees do not usually promise the members any benefits, for example, – they undertake merely to look after the beneficiaries' interests and their assets.

There is also no contractual relationship between the trustees and the employer, in relation to the management of the fund. This can be a problem, for example, where the employer sells part of the business, promises the purchaser a share of the fund in respect of the employees who are moving across – but does not attempt to obtain your consent first. If your actuary considers you would be paying too much to the purchaser's scheme, you may not be able to pay over what the employer wishes – what can you do?

A similar position arises where the employer fails to pay the contributions he should to the pension scheme. While you have to inform the authorities, are you also supposed to sue him for the contributions? In practice that is all but impossible if you are to keep on good terms as an employee. In any event the trustee may himself be the employer. There is no single solution in any of these cases – just find the best outside advice.

Member trustees

If you are already a trustee you may have a duty under the Pensions Act 1995 to ensure that scheme members have the opportunity to elect up to a third of the trustee board. In practice the employer will usually initiate the procedure, and you will be given guidance on how to respond. Such member trustees once elected or appointed are treated just like other trustees – and more importantly have the same obligations as other trustees. Member trustees should not use their new-found opportunities to negotiate for improvements, and must be particularly vigilant to ensure that they do not breach confidentialities which they become aware of because they are on the board.

10

PROTECTING YOURSELF

Old-age pensioner Stanley Dobek, 74, killed a cyclist with his car on Christmas Eve, switched off his lights and drove six miles home with the body sticking through the windscreen, state police said yesterday.

On the way back, he drove on the wrong side of the road in Lantana Florida, hit a truck and then careered into another vehicle.

It was being driven by an off-duty sheriff's deputy who chased him, joined by other motorists, shocked at the grim sight.

They watched as the retired company executive pulled the corpse the rest of the way through the windscreen and tried to stuff it completely under the car.

"I know nothing about the accident," he said when interviewed. "I've been to church."

Dobek, of Lake Worth, will be charged with either the manslaughter of 42-year-old John Davis, which carries a 15-year maximum jail sentence; or vehicular homicide which carries a possible five years' imprisonment.

The problem of "white tops," old folks with failing reflexes, impaired faculties or the effects of prescription drugs, let loose on the highways, is causing concern in Florida.

Several fatal accidents have been caused by stooped old ladies behind the wheels of big cars.

It is not helped by the fact that, in what is supposed to be paradise for retirees, there is little public transport.

'Cyclist's body driven 6 miles', Daily Telegraph, 31 December 1988

Introduction

In theory, being a trustee involves a great deal of responsibility – and potential liability. But in practice, you will normally be well protected against liability – and you should check that some of the protective devices, if not all, cover you. No one wants to be sued for a large sum of money because they tried to be helpful.

You will, of course, already have:

- taken and used professional advice,

- followed the documents,

- ensured protection is built into the documents,

- been reasonable,

- ensured that employers and trustees have no conflict of interest – and, if they have, obtained independent advice,

- kept your eye on the main principles, and avoided being distracted by technical details.

With all this, it is unlikely you will have done anything too terrible (ie committed a 'breach of trust') unless you have really been looking for trouble. And the horror stories which circulate trustees' association meetings about fines imposed by the Pensions Ombudsman or the potential penalties about to be imposed by the court under the Pensions Act 1995 are usually just those, ie stories. Nonetheless it is sensible to reduce the risk of liability, and there are a number of steps to take to do just that.

PROTECTION CHECKLIST

- Professional advice
- Trustee Act 1925
- Exoneration Clause
- Corporate Trustees
- Delegate functions
- Indemnity Clause
- Insurance

LOOKING FOR TROUBLE – THE SCARGILL CASE

Arthur Scargill the miners' leader, and one of the trustees of the Mineworkers' pension fund, had attempted to frustrate the investment plan of the Mineworkers' pension fund. He objected to the fund planning to invest in property in the United States (rather than in the UK) and in the oil industry (rather than in coal). The court considered that his views reflected those of his union rather than those he could be expected to hold as a trustee having the best financial interests of the members at heart.

Although he defended the case himself, rather than through lawyers, the expenses were considerable. The deed provided that such legal expenses would be reimbursed to trustees unless they resulted from 'wilful default' by the trustee. On an application for expenses to be paid by the fund, the court held that Mr Scargill had behaved with wilful default, and was refused his costs.

The deed

In most cases the deed will contain two vital clauses:

- An indemnity clause, which says that if you are sued, the employer will pick up the tab. Such a clause is only useful provided the employer stays in business; and

- An exoneration clause which exempts you from liability unless you have actually stolen the money.

Most modern deeds will contain these clauses, but some of the older documents may be deficient. These kind of clauses have recently been tested in the courts and found effective – even against fines imposed by the Pensions Ombudsman – although they cannot of course protect you against criminal fines or jail sentences if you steal the money, or civil penalties imposed by OPRA.

Insurance and defence unions

A few schemes now take out insurance against trustees' liability. It can be expensive, and it is not clear how effective it is in practice, since few claims have yet been made. In practice, unless you are very wealthy, few people will sue you personally since you are unlikely to be able to find a couple of million to compensate for investing wrongly in ENRON, or putting the fund's money with Barlow Clowes for example, although some beneficiaries may come after you with a shotgun. But the main risk is that you may have to find legal expenses to defend a claim which has no merit.

You should also consider whether you would like your fund (like many of the larger funds do) to join the Occupational Pensions Defence Union or equivalent. You should think very carefully about not joining (I declare an interest as an adviser to one!) since it gives protection not only while you are a trustee but also for an extended period after you have completed your service as trustee, which in many ways is the most exposed period.

The court

If a matter ever came to court the chances are it would excuse the trustees for errors which are reasonable. (Professional trustees, eg solicitors and actuaries, have higher standards of responsibility). In practice, the main problem for trustees is paying the legal costs. In most deeds, trustees are indemnified by the trust for legal costs. If not, trustees can ask the court, in a preliminary application, to allow their costs to be paid by the fund. It is highly unusual for the court to refuse; the only reported case is the *Scargill* case (see above).

Taking advice

The point of having advisers – investment managers, actuaries, pension fund managers, insurance companies, pensions consultants, accountants and administrators – is:

- first, because you cannot be expected to be an expert on everything – or even anything, and equally importantly,

- secondly, to have someone to blame if things go wrong.

Trust law expects pension fund trustees to have advisers, and judges will be a little sniffy if you do not. Passing the buck is one thing that pension fund trustees should specialise in.

The problem is that you should not blindly take the word of an adviser. If you genuinely feel it is wrong or inappropriate, either decline it (having thought carefully about it first) or find fresh advice. Blindly following advice will not excuse you.

Finally, just check who your advisers are acting for. If you are a trustee of an insured scheme, the actuary may be acting more for the insurance company than for you. And in a self-administered scheme the adviser may be acting for the employer, not the trustees. You need to check.

Criminal liability

Of course, if you were a criminal in the real sense you would not be reading this. But recent developments in the law mean that you may be committing criminal offences unwittingly, and in many of these cases, ignorance is no excuse. With the increasing belligerence of the Serious Fraud Office it might be very useful and sensible if your pension fund provided some form of criminal legal aid to help you defend yourself without you having to sell your house, against something you never even knew about. And with the criminal and near-criminal penalties imposed under the Pensions Act 1995 in some cases you cannot help but commit some minor infringement, which in most cases will be no more serious than a parking offence (which is also criminal).

The pension fund cannot pay your fines or civil penalties if any are imposed on you (although you can get your employer to indemnify you against payment of any civil penalties) nor can the pension fund buy insurance to protect you against such penalties.

Corporate trustees

One of the objects of pension fund design is to mitigate (reduce) the exposure of the trustees to legal liabilities.

One way of doing this is to have a company as a trustee, rather than individual people. This way any aggrieved member would have to sue the company, not a person. If he succeeded, any victory would by Pyrrhic, since the assets of the company would only be say £2.

Most legal opinion says that a trust company does not protect the directors of the company (ie you). But any protection, however modest, is useful, and while litigation is on the increase it is a course of action you should seriously think of taking. There are other advantages to having a company as trustee as well:

- it is easier to resign;

- there is no need to have repeated trust deeds every time a trustee changes,

but the drawbacks include:

- you have to file accounts every year;

- you acquire the responsibilities of directors under the Companies Acts; and

- you must comply with the other statutory requirements for companies.

The other trustees

You have to keep an eye on the other trustees – they can land you in it, and even if you had had nothing to do with what they did, the buck will stop with you. If you do not trust your other trustees, or have some other reason for being uncomfortable with their decision-making, either they or you should go. It is not a matter in which to be a wimp.

PART II

TRUSTEESHIP IN PRACTICE

What few of the books tell you, at least the conventional trustee training books, is what to do when faced with some of the day-to-day problems in running a pension fund, or the questions that are asked at a trustees' meeting.

This next section is intended to do just that. If you find that your problem is not discussed – write to us, and we'll try to make sure it comes out in the next edition.

It covers such areas as:

- what to do when the employer calls for a return of surplus;

- what to do if he goes bust;

- how to exercise discretions;

- the problems of take-overs and amalgamations.

This section does not pretend to have all the answers; every problem is personal to you and your fund. But it does try to mention some of the common difficulties – and suggests one or two ideas on how to approach their solution.

11

TRUSTEES' MEETINGS

Maxwell pension fund money was used to help finance the share support operation mounted in 1991 to boost the value of stock in Maxwell Communication Corporation, Mr Kevin Maxwell admitted to an Old Bailey jury yesterday . . .

During highly charged questioning by Mr Alan Suckling QC, Mr Maxwell said the £150M came from asset sales, cash flow, Maxwell Communication Corporation and the pension funds . . . Robert Maxwell had obtained legal advice that the operation was lawful, but he did not know from whom, Mr Kevin Maxwell said . . . Mr Kevin Maxwell agreed that he had never read the regulators' rule book on the role of the pension fund trustee. He delegated this responsibility to others, he said.

However he had seen his father run the pension funds for several years. 'That was my framework, not some external rule book,' he said.

Mr Maxwell admitted that he spent only about 30 minutes a week on pension fund business — less than he spent watching Oxford United play football. 'Do you regard that as disgraceful?' Mr Suckling asked. Mr Maxwell disagreed, but said in retrospect he would have acted differently.

John Mason, pension money 'was used to top up share price' Financial Times 2 November 1995

Introduction

In order to manage the pension fund, the trustees need to meet from time to time. There is no set frequency; smaller schemes might meet twice a year. Some very large schemes meet perhaps monthly, although it is difficult to know why; trustees are supposed to decide strategy rather than detail.

How the meetings run

You can run your meetings, with some exceptions, however you wish. But you must keep records of any meeting, including:

- the date, time and place

- the names of the trustees invited

- the names of the trustees present, and the names of those absent

- the names of anyone else who attended

- any decisions made

- whether any decision has been made since the previous meeting (with details, if a decision has been made).

In addition it is the trustees's duty to ensure that other records are maintained, covering members, contributions, receipts and payments, but in practice the administrator will be responsible for this on a day-to-day basis.

The records must be kept for six years.

The point of meetings

All but the smallest schemes will delegate most of the more trivial decisions to others. The point of most meetings is therefore:

- to supervise the administrators and others; and

- to exercise the discretions, which cannot be delegated.

It is crucial to keep proper minutes (not necessarily full ones), and to make sure the formalities are observed.

AGENDA

1. Minutes of the previous meeting – to approve
2. Investment manager's report – to approve
3. Scheme manager's report – to approve
4. Scheme accounts – to approve
5. Trustees' report – to approve
6. Actuarial report – to commission
7. Appointment of solicitors – beauty parade
8. Current developments – examination of impact on scheme of changes in the law and practice
9. Member communications – to approve
10. Scheme rule amendments – to approve
11. Individual discretions: early retirement; death-in-service payments; augmentations (improvements)
12. Any other business
13. Date of next meeting

Before the meeting takes place it is as well to check:

- who will be the chairman

- how decisions are taken, eg by majority vote – or do you have a veto

- how many trustees are needed to make a quorum

- whether resolutions have to be in writing

12

SURPLUSES (IN FINAL SALARY SCHEMES)

> The Times of Tuesday gives some very interesting figures as to the finances of the United States. The mighty work of 'getting rid of the surplus' to which the Republican Party has devoted itself for the last three years has been accomplished, and unless President Harrison can manage to effect economies under certain heads, there will actually be a deficit next year. The heroic scale on which the money has been "chucked away" may be gathered from the fact that the charge for pensions during the year ending June 30th was close on £25,000,000 – an increase since the previous year of some three millions sterling – and more than a third of the total annual disbursements of the nation.
>
> *The Spectator, 18 July 1891*

Introduction

Surpluses, despite collapsing stock markets in recent years, still exist in many schemes as a consequence of the booming stock markets in the 1990s, although for many funds deficits, as in the 1970s, are now the order of the day. Where there are surpluses, there is considerable debate about who owns them – whether they belong to the employer, the employees or even the Crown. They are only a real problem if your scheme is a 'final-salary' scheme; they do not usually form an issue where your scheme is a money-purchase (sometimes called a defined contribution) scheme.

The *employer* argues that in a 'balance-of-cost' scheme, ie a scheme where the employer promises to pay whatever is necessary after the employees have paid a fixed contribution, the surplus should be his. After all, he put money in to meet any deficit, and the reason the surplus has arisen is because of over-payment by him in the past.

The *employees* argue (supported by their unions) that the money should be theirs; after all it has resulted from the growth in value of 'their' money, on assets held in trust for their benefit.

The *Revenue* argues that some of it at least should be theirs, since they gave tax relief on it in the past.

The trustees role

The trustees should not have a view. First, much depends on what the deed says – some deeds absolutely prevent a repayment of money to the employer, and you may need to apply to the court to have the restriction lifted. Secondly, in all cases you must apply to the Occupational Pensions Regulatory Authority to repay money to the employer. And thirdly, the law is a little vague on some details as to how the money should be split if you receive a request for repayment from the employer.

In practice, a useful rule of thumb is to give say 40% to the taxman, 30% to the employer and 30% to the employee, or some similar split. A rather formal dance has to be performed to get to this position, and the trustees and the employer should have separate legal and actuarial representation. Both of you need to negotiate hard on a deal – and explore whether there are other options, or a combination of options. For example, you might be able to negotiate a mixture of a partial return of surplus, a contribution holiday, an increase in some benefits, or some other alternatives. Whatever you agree, receiving independent advice is crucial in all but relatively minor cases. The fact that the Inland Revenue has to agree to any deal, and may in fact do so, does not mean that it is a reasonable one for you as a trustee – it just means that it is reasonable for the Revenue, which is a very different thing.

The special case of insolvency

Where your employer has gone bust, different rules may apply; in some cases if the company is wound up before the scheme is, the balance must go to the Crown, because it is presumed there is no owner at all. This would be a great waste of the contributions, so painfully built up by employer and employee over the years, and could not only infuriate creditors but also your members.

In other cases, the liquidator may put in a claim either for the surplus, or even for all the contributions paid over the previous few years, arguing they were paid when the company was insolvent. The question of what to do when the company goes bust is dealt with elsewhere (see chapter 21).

WHAT TO CHECK ON AN APPLICATION FOR RETURN OF SURPLUS BY AN EMPLOYER

- Have you got your own independent actuary?
- Have you got an independent lawyer?
- What does the deed say should happen?
- Have you considered contribution holidays? benefit improvements? payments of tax?
- What do the members want or need?
- Are any benefit improvements fair across the board?
- Do you need an independent trustee?
- What can the employer do if you refuse to give him the money?
- Can you do a deal – ie improve benefits in exchange for agreeing to a return of surplus?
- What happens if the employer goes bust?
- Will the Revenue agree to the deal?
- Will OPRA agree to the deal?
- Who pays for the separate advice?

Walton J But what is called, in this connection, a surplus, having no existence in reality, represents, in a case of the present nature, what may be termed temporary surplus funding by the employing company. (Re Imperial Food Ltd's Pension Scheme [1986] 2 All ER 812)

Warner J One cannot, in my opinion, in construing a provision in the rules of a 'balance of cost' pension scheme relating to a surplus, start from an assumption that any surplus belongs morally to the employer. (Mettoy Pension Trustees Ltd v Evans [1990] Pensions Law Reports para 177)

Scott J Accordingly, in my judgment, if any part of the surplus has derived from employees' contributions or from the funds transferred from the pension schemes of other companies, that part of the surplus devolves as bona vacantia (Davis v Richards & Wallington Industries [1990] Pensions Law Reports para 150)

Millet J I think it would be a pity to waste these surpluses by not ensuring that some part of them are used to pay the lawyers (Re Courage Group's Pension Scheme [1987] 1 WLR 495)

You pays your money.............

13

CHANGES TO THE SCHEME

A man who lied about his age 36 years ago while courting an older woman yesterday found himself in court after love turned sour and the woman disclosed the truth.

For years Brian Sale kept the secret that he was six years his wife's junior and not three years older as he had told her to win her heart. On his wedding day in 1955 his age was recorded as 29 and that of his wife Gwen as 26, and, aided by his mature physique and by falsifying documents, he was able to carry on the deception throughout his life.

He did so even when he took early retirement because of an injury and received over £11,000 in pension payments to which he was not legally entitled, Elwyn Evans, for the prosecution told Swansea crown court.

Lin Jenkins, Law catches the young pretender, Times, 22 August 1991

Introduction

A pension scheme is a dynamic, organic beast – and needs to change continually to meet changes in law and the needs of the employers and employees.

What does not change is the obligation, having invested the assets to the best of your ability, to pay the benefits, as set down in the rules and announcements.

In practice you will not do this yourself – the insurance company, pensions consultant or administrator will do this for you. But there may be cases where the wrong amount has been paid – or the wrong person has been paid – or the records do not match the claim.

It is not your job to change the benefits or improve them – unless the deed says so. And even so, you usually have to do it with the consent of the employer.

Some of the more common problems that arise include:

- Should you count time on strike as part of pensionable service?

- Should you count maternity leave as part of pensionable service?

- Should the benefits be paid monthly, quarterly or for some other period?

- How do you check that the beneficiary is still alive?

- How do you check that a person claiming to be a widow was married to the dead member?

These kind of benefit checks, including who is eligible to join and how, are normally agreed by the employer rather than the trustee. And it may be that revisions to the scheme and its documents are needed to meet changing social circumstances.

Benefit improvements

Benefit improvements can arise:

- from a decision of the employer, perhaps negotiated with the trade union;

- as a way of dealing with part of a surplus;

- where increased contributions are agreed; or

- where required by law.

In almost all cases they arise from employees' negotiations with the employer – not with the trustees. Unless a deal has to be done about some surplus, you will not be called upon to decide who gets what – but if you are, you need to remember to treat all groups on an equal footing (members, retired members, deferred pensioners and the rest). They do not have to get equal benefits – you can treat different groups differently, but you need to be satisfied that the split is fair in the circumstances.

14

TRADE UNIONS

When Denning had been transferred to the King's Bench Division he had been nominated by the Lord Chancellor to hear Pensions Appeals. He thought that the Minister and Pensions Tribunals had been applying the wrong principles and took steps to put them right. The Minister had put upon the applicant the burden of proving that his injury or illness was due to war service. Denning changed the burden of proof. He held that if a man or woman were fit when he or she joined up and unfit when discharged the burden was on the Minister to prove that the injury or illness was not due to war service. The slogan was "Fit for service, fit for pension".

Edmund Heward, Lord Denning, A Biography,
Weidenfeld and Nicholson, 1991

Introduction

Trade unions nowadays play much less of a role in industrial relations than they used to – but as their influence has waned, so has their proficiency improved, certainly in the pensions arena.

Many union representatives still find it difficult to understand that pension trusteeship is not a bargaining position, or that surpluses could ever have a home with an employer; but at the same time some unions have made significant contributions to the understanding of their members about pensions and can negotiate, over the wages table, about pensions with the best of them. Some even retain actuaries and lawyers to act on their behalf, increasing the skills resource even further.

Representation and consultation

At present there is no law in the UK that unions are entitled to representation on the boards of trustees of pension funds. It was suggested some years ago but the suggestion has failed to catch the public imagination.

Nonetheless, trade unions are entitled to be consulted on a number of matters, and are entitled to particular information about their members' pension schemes – although not of course about individual details of each member.

15

DIVORCE, POLYGAMY AND SAME-SEX RELATIONSHIPS

A hoaxer has fooled dozens of hardened IRA men into believing they will be paid a pension for their long-term terrorist activities. The IRA has launched an internal inquiry into the redundancy notice ruse, which has infuriated and embarrassed some of the most feared gunmen in the Irish Republic.

IRA volunteers across Eire have been sent notices informing them pensions are available as part of the political settlement with the British Government.

The notices state that the IRA is trying to establish the pension rights for each volunteer and ex-volunteer and that a trust fund has been set up to administer the pay-outs. An attached form invites applications based on military service. Each claimant is asked to list his active service, including ambushes, bank raids or intelligence work.

Last night a Republican source in Tipperary said many of the men who received the fake worms had actually applied for pensions. He said 'One man even outlined his marriage breakdown and the trauma caused to his family by his IRA involvement. Another described how he imported Lee Enfield rifles in the Forties. Others were indignant that they did not receive application forms.'

Chester Stern, Mail on Sunday, 22 January 1995

Introduction

Most pension schemes are established to protect the income in retirement of the employee – and his or her family.

In recent years, however, pension rights have been seen as just another property right, and one which should be able to be dealt with by the courts if the member divorces.

Divorce

Accordingly the courts now have power, if the parties cannot make alternative arrangements, to order that at retirement some or all of the pension and/or any lump sum is paid to the spouse.

In addition the court can direct trustees to pay any death-in-service benefit to a former spouse of a member, overriding the usual trustees' discretion. You should not do this without a copy of the court order, and it is the former spouse's duty to keep you informed of any change of address.

At the end of 2000 the courts were given power to order a transfer value to be paid to a spouse, thus diminishing the rights of the member at divorce, rather than at retirement.

The only job of a trustee is to ensure that the scheme administrator has systems which can cope with complying with these orders.

Polygamy

There is no obligation on a private pension scheme to pay a pension to two (or more) surviving spouses, but most schemes, nowadays, have power to split the benefits as the trustees think fit if a member leaves several spouses.

There are special rules for state benefits, but an occupational scheme does not have to follow those rules.

Same-sex relationships

In the United States it is increasingly common to provide survivor's benefits for same-sex relationships. In this country it is rare but increasing, and the Inland Revenue changed the rules to make it easier to do so.

In some cases scheme rules allow trustees to use their discretion to pay benefits, but they have to be satisfied that there has been financial or other dependency. It is not certain whether trustees can apply their own views to the application of their discretion in such cases.

16

RELATIONSHIP WITH THE STATE SCHEME

Claude's been in pensions all his life. When he retires next year he'll collect a knighthood. He's got a Wates house in Surrey and 10 lines in WHO's WHO. He is one of those 'Beveridge Boys', who took the 6.30 train in the '50's with a black bowler hat and talked enthusiastically about false teeth and free specs. Claude's a retiring chap. But last week, he threw himself across a committee table and wrestled the PM to the floor. Has he gone mad?

Michael Hastings, A Dream of People,
Royal Shakespeare Company, 1990

Introduction

As the benefits offered by the state scheme (through both the basic pensions and the SERPS arrangements) decline in value, the relationship between private schemes and the state arrangements becomes more important.

One of the more important relationships concerns contracting-out (see Bluffer's Guide). This subject is one of the great turn-offs of any cocktail party conversation, and you should not spend too much time worrying about it.

If your scheme is not contracted-out, breathe a sigh of relief and skip this Chapter.

If your scheme is contracted-out, do not agonise whether it is the right or wrong thing. The decision to contract-out or not is a matter for the employer, not the trustees. Once he has made the decision, the job of the trustee is to comply with it.

Complexity

Contracted-out schemes are a little more complicated than even ordinary schemes:

- They have to collect contributions in relation to what would otherwise be national insurance payments from the employer and employee – and therefore there is additional supervision and form-filling and additional rules have to be agreed with the National Insurance Contributions Office;

- They have to file forms with the National Insurance Contributions Office every year to show they are solvent and have not invested the money wrongly;

- They have to pay special transfer payments when members move, and need to maintain separate records and to pay 'requisite benefits' (ie good enough benefits) which need to be monitored.

All this is a matter for the administrators and not for you. Pass on to other more exciting matters.

17

EQUAL TREATMENT

She got out of her mosquito netting and took a wooden chest out of the closet, with a packet of letters arranged by date and held together by a rubber band. She located the advertisement of a law firm which promised quick action on war pensions......

The colonel read the clipping dated two years before. He put it in the pocket of his jacket which was hanging behind the door.

"The problem is that to change lawyers you need money."

"Not at all," the woman said decisively. "You write them telling them to discount whatever they want from the pension itself when they collect it. It's the only way they'll take the case."

So Saturday afternoon the colonel went to see his lawyer...

"I warned you it would take more than a few days," said the lawyer when the colonel paused..... "It's been that way for fifteen years," the colonel answered......" We'll I've decided to take action."

The lawyer waited. "Such as?"

"To change lawyers."

A mother duck, followed by several little ducklings, entered the office. The lawyer sat up to chase them out. "As you wish, Colonel, he said......

"My son worked all his life," said the colonel. "My house is mortgaged. That retirement law has been a lifetime pension for lawyers."

"Not for me," the lawyer protested. "Every last cent has gone for my expenses."

The colonel suffered at the thought that he had been unjust.

Gabriel Garcia Marquez, No One Writes to the Colonel, Picador, 1979

Introduction

There was a time when you could hardly open a newspaper (even the Sun) without being assailed by articles on the equal treatment for men and women in pension schemes. Why was there so much agitation? And is it still anything for you, as a trustee, to worry about?

Equal treatment

In relation to equal treatment the problem is a very simple one. In 1942 the government (after pressure from the TUC) agreed to change the then retirement age from 70 to 65 for men and 60 for women, most private or company schemes followed the same pattern. But nowadays:

- women object to being forced to retire before men,

- UK law makes it illegal to have different retirement ages in the contract of employment, and

- European Community law (following a famous case called *Barber v GRE*) now makes it illegal to have different pension ages in the pension scheme.

The problem for trustees is: how can the you reconcile the need to have the same retirement/pension age at work with different state pension ages?

If the retirement age is equalised at, say, 65, then women can complain that they now have to work another five years before they can get their pension. If the age is equalised at say 60, then men will complain that they have five fewer years to earn a living and acquire additional pension rights.

The *bad news* is that there is no perfect answer; whatever is done to try and reform the situation, someone will suffer. The *good news* is that the problem is not one for the trustees; it is the employer who has to sort out the problem. From May 1990, the retirement date for men and women had to be the same; but retrospective benefits do not have to be granted to members or former members of the scheme, or even pensioners, so that the fund has not been put in peril.

The trustee's only job is to keep a watching brief. Apart from some minor technicalities which have yet to be ironed out, for most pension schemes equal treatment is no longer a problem, except that it is required that retirement ages should now be the same for men and women, as should the entry requirements (for example, for part-timers and full-timers, where most of the part-timers are women).

Bridging pensions (ie money paid to men who retire after 60 but before 65, to take account of the fact that they do not draw a state pension, unlike the women) are legal, although there was a major legal battle about them. In due course, as the state pension ages are equalised over the next twenty years (to 65 for both genders), the problem will disappear.

Race discrimination

It is as illegal to discriminate in pension schemes on racial grounds as it is on sex grounds. That is not to say that pension schemes are obliged to reflect differing social customs for different groups of members, such as those groups who possess more than one wife, or groups who have strong views on investment morality. But racial discrimination is as wrong in pensions as it is anywhere else.

Age discrimination

Unlike in the United States, there is no law outlawing age discrimination – and in a way pension schemes are discriminatory on age everywhere you look. A law against age discrimination comes into effect at the end of 2006.

18

EARLY LEAVERS

Irving's first words to me were "Hitler pensioned the widows of the hanged 1944 bomb plotters – and the officers of the Czech army after his takeover." I said, "My dear fellow, when my country, Austria-Hungary, was shattered into six pieces and the age-old all highest Arch-House of Hapsburg chucked out, the Austro-Hungarian Finance Minister got on a train to Warsaw, became Polish Finance Minister, and didn't miss a single pension contribution." Pensions offend the English sense of order because you don't have to toady once you get your secure indexed pension. But in normal countries, even under Hitler, pensions have the status which payments to royals and landowners have in England – to be paid before all other things. Curiously those English who rather admire Hitler – maybe a third of the population – often praise his welfare system which, if proposed here, would lead to a universally applauded MI5 coup against the red threat.

George Stern, review of David Irving, Hitler's War, Literary Review,
December 1991

Preservation and what it means

Until only a few years ago, if you left your employer any time before your normal retirement age, all the pension you had earned could be forfeited. The reason was that most pension schemes confiscated your rights if you did not retire whilst in the employer's employment.

Nowadays, there are laws against this; they are called, in the UK, 'preservation'. In the United States, they call it 'vesting' and Ralph Nader, the campaigner against unsafe cars, also wrote a less-well-known book exposing such companies as Studebaker and Woolworths, who promised fine pensions but paid them relatively infrequently. His efforts changed US law as well.

There were (and are) some problems with preservation. It only applies to the rights you have earned at the date of leaving — not the date of retirement. And the benefits, until recently, did not have to be index-linked in any way. This particular problem, ie inadequate preservation at a time when funds were building up surpluses, led to a highly critical Press, and after some years the law has been changed. Poor transfer values and poor preservation have been one of the weak spots of occupational schemes (and allowed the proponents of personal pensions to insert a wedge into their bedrock); nowadays the position is much improved, and personal pensions offer very little to critics of poor preservation.

Transfers

All members have a right not only to leave the scheme at any time, but to transfer their rights to some other arrangement when they have left employment. They can move it to:

- another occupational scheme (if it will take them);

- an insurance company (under either an s32 or a personal pension);

- a building society;

- a bank;

- a unit trust;

if they think it worthwhile.

The right to transfer

The right can be exercised at any time up to a year before retirement, and you have to give a member details of his transfer options. Whether it is worth the member's while is one of the great unknowns. In practice they will have been sold by some salesman some personal pension, which in reality is probably unlikely to match the benefits offered by the occupational pension. This is a problem which has been much reduced by vast publicity about pensions mis-selling in the last few years, and scheme members are very much less likely to find salesmen encouraging moves away from occupational schemes nowadays.

Nonetheless, if a member does wish to leave, there's not much you can do to dissuade him apart from:

- making sure your own documents are clear and sensible 'selling' documents which set out the advantages of your scheme; and

- offering a personal pensions protection certificate for the salesman to sign (see page 129)

In any event it is not your function to sell one scheme or arrangement or another – you are not your members' financial adviser. At the same time, you probably have a duty to explain to your members how they can lose by entering into personal pension arrangements without proper advice – which is all but impossible to get, since commission-based systems are still the rule.

The value of transfers

The value of the transfer payment is set down by law as a minimum; you may have the right to offer more in particular circumstances, remembering to try not to discriminate between one group of members and another.

Information about transfers

Members are entitled to information about their transfer values at least once a year on request. You will not normally charge, although it can be an expensive exercise doing the calculations.

WHY TRANSFER PAYMENTS FROM ONE SCHEME DON'T BUY YEARS OF SERVICE IN THE NEXT SCHEME

Suppose

- you are in a scheme earning 1/60 of your final salary for each year of service.

- you work for twenty years for Company Smith, and another twenty years for Company Jones.

- your salary has improved from £1,000 pa to £10,000 in the first twenty years, and from £12,000 to £20,000 in the last twenty years.

- Each company operates an identical pension scheme.

Then

- in the first 20 years you will have earned rights to a pension, to be taken at say age 65, as follows:

- 20 years at 1/60th of final salary (in this case, not actual final salary, but salary at leaving the company) for each year of service is the same as

$$20 \times 1/60 \times £10,000 = £3,333 \text{ pension pa at age } 65$$

And

- in the second 20 years, you will have earned rights to a pension as follows:

- 2o years at 1/60 of final salary (in this your actual final salary) for each year of service, which means

$$20 \times 1/60 \times £20,000 = £6,666 \text{ pension pa at age } 65$$

Together the two pensions are therefore £9,999.

But

If you had spent 40 years with Scheme Jones, the sum would have been:

- $40 \times 1/60 \times £20,000 = £13,333$

cont'd on next page

Consequence

- By changing employers midstream, you have lost a substantial pension. Why? The answer is that the first employer assumes that your final pension is not your actual final pension but the pension you earned when you left him. Is it fair? Well, the first employer argues that he cannot be responsible for your future rapid earnings growth once you have left him. And the new employer, when you bring a pension only worth £6,666 a year into his scheme argues that it is not his responsibility to make up another £3,000 a year of pension for time when you were not working for him. It's just one of those conundrums.

- Nonetheless, unless you are a very frequent mover to different employers, the system is still a better one, for most people, than a personal pension, with all its overheads and surrender penalties. Just try moving a personal pension between one provider and another and see what transfer value you get!

Why the transfer won't buy added years

You would think it would be sensible, if you had saved with one occupational scheme for say ten years, you could move the transfer rights to another scheme, and it would buy you also ten years' worth. In some cases it will – especially in the transfer club of the Civil Service and similar schemes.

But the way in which occupational schemes work doesn't operate like that.

The reason is that there are (at least) three ways of working out your rights in a scheme, which involve the way in which a scheme works. A pension scheme is not a savings pot (like a personal pension) – and it is not an insurance arrangement, like a life policy that pays only if something adverse happens. It is something in between – and just because it is difficult to define, does not mean that it is a con.

It works by calculating, as a group of people, what the life expectancy of the individual members of that group will be (and their dependants). The contributions take account of future inflation, future salary growth, future earnings in the fund, and any tax. If any of those assumptions prove incorrect (as they inevitably will), the contribution structure will later need adjustment.

Unfortunately the only way we can explain it is by looking at some calculations (these are the only calculations in the book).

The three transfer values

There are many different ways of calculating transfer values. This section looks at just three of the main ones:

- the discontinuance valuation;

- the past service valuation; and

- the share of surplus.

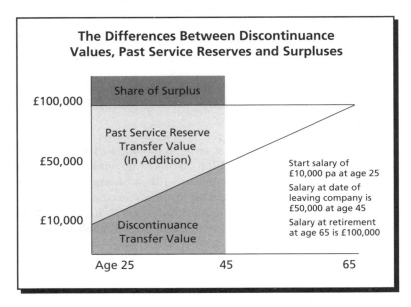

The Differences Between Discontinuance Values, Past Service Reserves and Surpluses

Share of Surplus

Past Service Reserve Transfer Value (In Addition)

Discontinuance Transfer Value

£100,000

£50,000

£10,000

Age 25   45   65

Start salary of £10,000 pa at age 25

Salary at date of leaving company is £50,000 at age 45

Salary at retirement at age 65 is £100,000

The *discontinuance transfer value* assumes your final salary to be the one you are earning at the date you leave the employer or the scheme. It therefore does not include assumptions as to your future salary increases, either because of inflation, career progression, or increases for longer service. It is the minimum transfer value, and is regulated by the 'Transfer Regulations'. It is the usual basis of calculating your transfer value when you leave before retirement.

The *past service reserve transfer value* is the same as the discontinuance transfer value, but builds-in the reserves that have been set aside to take account of expectations about your future salary growth. It is the usual basis employed when there is a bulk transfer of many members or employees to another scheme (perhaps because of a take-over).

The *share of fund* is sometimes looked at where there is a surplus; it can result in a transfer value more than those arising under the other two methods (where there is a surplus) or less (where there is a deficit).

19

TAKE OVERS AND MERGERS

The inevitability of disaster gripped Buddy's stomach like a tick when he heard the word liquidate. He felt solitary in his terror and humiliation. Bud turned his eyes upon himself and looked at his body as if he were filthy. Was his father right after all? Betrayal and disintegration hung in the air like a dark cloud before Buddy's eyes, as Burnside answered the bankers.

"Guaranteed! No sweat . . . we already got the Bleezer brothers lined up to build condos where the hangars are. We can lay off the planes with Mexicano. Midcontinental Air is drooling to get the slots and routes. What's the problem? It's done."

Barnes passed a formal looking spreadsheet to the commercial bankers.

"This is the price tag on the 737s, the gates, the hangars, the routes . . . We got it all nailed down to the typewriters."

Torment, shame, and self-mockery exploded inside Buddy like a cancer. *So this was hell*, he thought. Burnside's voice sounded distorted to him in the background as he detailed the dismemberment of Bluestar.

"The beauty of it is the overfunded pension fund. Gekko gets the seventy-five million in there. Fifty million buys him the minimum annuities' protection for six thousand employees, and he walks away with the rest. All in all, he'll net sixty to seventy million. Not bad for a month's work." He turned to Buddy. "Your man did his homework, Fox . . . you're gonna have a short executive career. Now he'll really start believing he's Gekko the Great!"

Kenneth Lipper, Wall Street, 1988

Introduction

A major concern for companies who may be the subject of unwelcome takeovers is the pensions position. Target companies need to ensure that the surpluses (if any) in their scheme are not 'in play' – and that the benefits will not be reduced by any future owner. This section gives the background to the problem, and suggests some practical steps.

Background

There are two main problems when bids are made for a target company, so far as pensions are concerned:

- **surpluses** – how is the surplus to be dealt with, and can it be recovered by the purchaser to mitigate the purchase price; and

- **benefits** – will the benefits, (especially the discretionary benefits like post-retirement increases), be continued after the takeover.

Because of these problems, and others, the now abolished Occupational Pensions Board was commissioned in 1988 to produce a report, *Protecting Pensions*, on what happened to pensions in such cases.

Following the OPB Report, and the Goode Committee Report following the Maxwell Affair, changes in the law were introduced (in the Pensions Act 1995) and schemes and members now enjoy an enhanced degree of protection; nonetheless such protection is limited, and some companies may need to take extra precautions.

Existing surpluses

Existing surpluses normally arise:

- through excessive employer contributions;

- higher than expected returns on the pension fund assets;

- higher than expected staff-turnover (perhaps through redundancy programmes);

or a combination of all three.

Once in the scheme however, much of it must be used to enhance benefits.

At one time surpluses were an attractive prize for predators — and changes to the accountancy rules and the 'Disclosure Regulations' (information for members and others) made them more visible to shareholders and other interested parties. But recovery of surplus by a predator is now much more difficult than before:

- there is a tax charge of 35% on any such recovery;

- trust law requires (normally) that some of the surplus must be used to enhance benefits if any is returned to the employer; and

- limited indexation of benefits must be applied before surplus can be returned;

- the consent of the Occupational Pensions Regulatory Authority is required before any payment is made.

For these and other reasons, surpluses are much less attractive to predators than they used to be.

Expectations

Most pension schemes give 'expectations' of benefits as well as promises. For example, members can confidently expect in most cases that they will receive their formula pension (eg 2/3rds of final salary after 40 years). But such benefits as cost-of-living increases, or other benefit improvements are usually at the discretion of the trustees – often subject to the permission of the employer. While in most cases such permission is given as a matter of course, when the employer changes, such expectations may also change, even though there is enough money in the kitty to meet those expectations.

There are 'bulk transfer' rules which apply where groups of employees are moved to a purchaser's pension scheme which protect many of these expectations.

Practice

Most of the practical problems are those of the employer, not the trustees. But as a trustee you need to understand the employer's options, so that you can exercise any discretions available, for example whether to pay a bulk transfer payment in respect of a group of employees who have left to join another company pension scheme.

Employer's concerns include:

Changing the balance of power between the employer and trustee:

- The employer often has power to reduce, suspend or terminate contributions, ie take a 'contribution holiday'. This is a dangerous weapon in the hands of a predator, but amending the deed to take this right away might not be acceptable to the employer.

- The benefits can usually only be increased with the consent of the employer. Taking that consent away is an obvious way to protect the trustees and members, but may be too high a price for the existing employer.

- The trustees can usually be changed by the employer. Some schemes now have permanent 'independent trustees', but entrenching all the trustees in this way is usually unacceptable.

- The advisers can usually be changed by the employer; but different advisers can produce different levels of surplus, for example.

Introducing triggers ie clauses which only take effect if there is a change in the control of the employer. The problem with such triggers is that they may take effect even on a friendly change:

- Changing the deeds to forbid returns of surplus to an employer; this is not totally predator proof;

- Limiting the power of amendment of the deed by the trustees or employer, leaving control with the trustees who cannot be displaced;

- Increasing the pensions automatically to Revenue maxima on a winding-up or other trigger event.

As a trustee, your options will vary widely, depending on the position of the employer, the rules of the scheme and the expectations of the members.

Some employers (that is companies quoted on the Stock Exchange) will need to make changes to the deed and rules to avoid or reduce the impact of the Takeover Code (Rule 21). But these changes cannot be made where a bid is in progress or is imminent. Any changes made must also, of course, be in the shareholders' interest.

Requests for transfer payments

If you get requests for transfer payments, you should comply with them as soon as possible; if you delay there could be penalties. It is also sensible to advise anyone who requests a transfer payment to take some independent advice (ie not from someone who is commission-hungry).

20

WINDING-UP THE SCHEME

> It was almost midday. Her stomach was beginning to rumble. She ignored it for as long as possible then took a piece of bread out of her pocket and chewed on it. It would have to last until the evening; she could only afford one meal a day. She'd managed to save very little from the small pension the War Office had arranged for her, and most of that had gone on the train and ferry fare.
>
> *Clare Francis, Night Sky, Pan, 1984*

Introduction

You may need, in exceptional circumstances, to:

- *close the scheme*, usually if the employer demands it, by refusing to admit new members; or

- *freeze the scheme*, where, usually because the employer fails to pay any contributions due, or he goes bust, and there are no further contributions being paid to the scheme.

In both those cases what you will need to do is usually called 'winding-up', and there are likely to be extensive instructions in the deed on the steps to take.

What winding-up means

Winding-up does not necessarily mean the end of the scheme.
You often have a choice:

- Buy annuities or deferred annuities for all the members, and if
  there is anything left in the kitty, pay it back to the employer,
  and wind-up the trusts.

- Keep investing the income, and pay the benefits as they arise.
  You can run the scheme as is for another sixty years. This
  method is useful especially where the scheme has a surplus
  and for some reason it is not appropriate to pay it back to the
  employer. The bad news is somebody has to look after it for all
  that time, but that may not be an onerous job.

The tontine

Strictly, tontines are illegal, but they still arise in pension funds. A
tontine is a kind of bet, originally common amongst miners. Each
miner put five bob in the pot, and the one who survived the
longest scooped the pool. There was a great temptation to pull
the odd pit-prop, and so tontines are no longer permitted.

However in a pension fund, the member who lives the longest
could do just that. If there is a surplus in the kitty, and he is the
only surviving member, by using a cunning device called The Rule
in Saunders v Vautier, he could close the trust, and take all the
money (there may be some tax to pay).

While theoretically possible, in practice it is difficult to achieve –
you need all the beneficiaries to agree to this, and getting
unanimous agreement in pensions is something close to impossible.

21

WHEN YOUR EMPLOYER GOES BUST

> Another side of Maxwell's character that he has succeeded in hiding totally from public view enables him to be an exceptionally able chairman of committees, the best in my personal experience . . . The *Mirror* Pensions Board consists of half management, half trade union nominees. Maxwell, as chairman, has the casting vote. The balance is therefore tipped, as it always was, in favour of the management, but his conduct of the meetings was impeccable in my experience as a board member. When he does not hold all the aces, he will listen, persuade and respond.
>
> *Bob Edwards [former editor, Sunday Mirror], Goodbye, Fleet Street,*
> *Jonathan Cape, 1988*
>
> He could never be trusted. Anyone who knew Maxwell knew he could not be trusted. And anyone who says otherwise is a craven liar. I remember people telling me that if he could get his hands on the pension fund he would . . . in the end the pension fund was run by Maxwell and his lickspittles and the trustees were kept in the dark.
>
> *Bob Edwards [former editor, Sunday Mirror], the Sun,*
> *6 December 1991*

Introduction

When the employer goes bust the pension problems are usually the last thing on your mind – getting a new job is probably the priority.

Nonetheless the sad occasion can be seen, pensions-wise, as an opportunity as well as a problem.

First check the deed – the scheme may be automatically wound-up if the employer goes into receivership or liquidation. Receivership means the company still trades, but the company is run by a receiver, usually appointed by the bank. A liquidation means the company has finally failed – and no longer trades.

Independent trustee

In any case, the insolvency practitioner (ie the administrator, the receiver or the liquidator) by law has to ensure that there is an *independent trustee* of the fund. This does not mean that you are not independent, but there may be great pressure on you to do things you do not, in your heart, agree with (such as paying some surplus back to the liquidator). So the law now says that you must have some help in the person of an independent trustee. There are several firms, often experienced pensions lawyers, that now offer this service. You should liaise with the insolvency practitioner to ensure that the independent trustee is one whom you feel is appropriate for your fund. If you already have an independent trustee, there is no need for the insolvency practitioner to become involved.

These trustees will charge, but their duty is to the beneficiaries and they are trained to withstand the sort of pressures that liquidators bring to recover funds for the creditors.

Telling the members

One of the simplest yet most crucial jobs is to tell the members what is happening, or even that nothing is happening. Members and pensioners will at that stage all feel lonely and unloved, and need to know that someone is looking after their interests. They may not be receiving their full benefits or indeed any benefits at all if the pensions were paid through the payroll system. There may be some hiccups, where, for example, money has gone missing and there is no Guaranteed Minimum Pension (GMP — see appendix I) being paid. It may not be your fault (and the

Government will eventually pay up where the GMP funds have disappeared) but you will get the blame if you do not explain what is going on.

Deficits

If there is a deficit in the fund, there may not be enough money in the kitty to pay the benefits – or there may be money owing to the fund. You have one or two tasks to do (or to find someone to do them) including:

- claiming against the redundancy fund for payments which have been deducted by the employer but not handed over to the pension fund;

- claiming against the employer for any unpaid contributions – although in practice the employer will have little funds left after paying preferential creditors (such as the Inland Revenue) to pay you or your fund;

- claim against the employer for any remaining deficit; and if there is still not enough;

- claim against the Pensions Compensation Fund operated by the Pensions Ombudsman if there has been fraud.

There is also the remote possibility of a claim against the government for failing to introduce (as required under European Union law) a wider compensation fund.

22

MEMBERS' RIGHTS

> Friday July 30: Our family went to Pandora's house to discuss what was involved in looking after Bert while we are on holiday.
>
> Bert grumbled all the way through the meeting. He's never a bit grateful for anything you do for him. Sometimes I wish he would go and live in the Alderman Cooper Sunshine Home. My mother gave this list to Pandora's mother:
>
> 1   He will only drink out of the George V Coronation Cup . . .
>
> 2   He'll accuse you of fiddling him out of his pension. Ignore him
>
> *Sue Townsend, The Growing Pains of Adrian Mole, Methuen, 1985*

Introduction

As was discussed earlier beneficiaries (including both the employer and the members) have a considerable interest in the well-being of the fund which guarantees the payment of their benefits. So it is not surprising that members and other beneficiaries have a few rights over the management of it.

These rights are quite wide:

- Information

- A right to be dealt with fairly

- Rights to transfer payments to other schemes

- A right to leave the scheme

- A right to nominate up to a third of the trustees.

Not all rights apply to all members; for example 'deferred pensioners' (ie those who have some pension rights under the scheme but are no longer employees) may have no legal right to play a part in nominating trustees. And some of these rights are often only of peripheral interest to trustees; but the ones that often come up in practice include:

Membership

The right to be a member is usually set out in the deed and rules; it may be subject to the employer's approval. The right to resign is a statutory right – no-one can be compelled to be a member of the scheme, although this right to resign is looked on with a jaundiced view by colleagues in other Member States of the European Community. It may be that membership of some kind of occupational scheme will become compulsory in years to come.

Information

Members have always had a right to information about their scheme; that right is now enshrined in regulations, has been extended to their dependants, and is more easily enforceable (in theory at least).

Transfers

Members have a right, when they leave, to transfer their rights to another scheme (or to an insurance company, building society or bank in some cases). There is a minimum value related to the years-of-service and the level-of-benefits (in a final salary scheme) to which they are entitled. In some cases this may be unfair to people who stay – whose rights may be less well protected, especially in an underfunded scheme.

Equal treatment

Nowadays equal treatment covers a multitude of areas, from sex equality and racial equality to equality between different groups, such as pensioners and employees. The duty of trustees to behave fairly between these groups varies depending on whether the duty is statutory (as it is where sex equality is concerned) or equitable (as it is where discrimination between age groups is concerned).

The members and the employer

Recently the courts have indicated that members and perhaps others are entitled to fair treatment not only from the trustees – but also from the employer. Where the employer has a right to limit the trustees' actions – for example, when considering whether or not to give a pension on the grounds of serious ill-health – he must now use such powers as though he were a trustee himself, and not merely an employer trying to save overheads.

This recent development in the law is not without controversy, and it is an area which is still unsettled; nonetheless, trustees need to be aware of the new duties of employers.

23

GIVING ADVICE

You might like to send birthday greetings to Jack Bendon, 75 on Sunday, who may well be the ultimate life insurance salesman. Mr Bendon is clearly all heart. He has to thank for this, most notably, Mr Magdi Yacoub, the eminent cardiothoracic surgeon. Mr Bendon has been fitted with, in turn, two pacemakers; more recently he has had heart by-pass surgery at Harefield Hospital, in Hillingdon. And then, what did he do? Picked himself up and promptly sold Prof Yacoub a personal pension, didn't he? Mr Bendon, a senior associate with Abbey Life, said yesterday: "I'm just a very ordinary salesman but I have a bit of nerve. I was in the wholesale fruit business for 35 years....."

Diary, The Guardian, 20 December 1990

Introduction

Trustees like to help. They wouldn't be trustees unless they were that kind of person.

So when requests come in for some help from a member, it is natural to try and respond.

In most cases, this is fine. But there are one or two areas where caution is needed. Clearly it would be foolish to advise on legal or actuarial matters – trustees are not usually lawyers or actuaries.

But what about a member who asks for help on whether he should stay in the fund or take a personal pension? Or whether it is better for him to take a commuted lump sum, or a pension, when he knows he has an incurable disease?

The law now requires that advice on 'investment matters' can only be given by an authorised person – usually insurance brokers and the like. It is unlikely you are authorised, and you commit a serious offence if you advise in such cases – and the liability for getting it wrong is also high.

But occupational pension schemes themselves are not considered to be investments – so you can advise quite freely on their benefits and advantages – and you should do so, since no-one else will.

You might like, however, to help your members by offering them a protection certificate against over-ambitious personal pensions salesmen. One is shown below. However the rules on selling personal pensions have been tightened up in recent years, and few of your members nowadays will face the problem of aggressive personal pensions salesmen.

The state pension

Giving advice on the state pension is a highly skilled art; it is better practice just to refer inquiries to a series of DWP leaflets many of which are well-drafted, or to the Age Concern guide (see FURTHER READING).

PERSONAL PENSION PROTECTION CERTIFICATE

To our members:

Before you sign up for a personal pension (and resign from your company pension scheme) you should get the salesman to sign this certificate. You do not have to, but it will ensure that the deal he offers you is the right one for you.

I_____

of_____

independent intermediary for / tied agent for / employee of

_____

[pension provider]

HEREBY CERTIFY

to _____

of_____

[the member]

that in accordance with

- the best advice rules; and
- the know your customer rules

I have

- examined the provisions of the _____ Retirement Benefits Scheme and in particular
  - its history of benefit increases
  - its actuarial assumptions as to future growth
  - its benefit structure
  - its overheads

- considered your personal financial needs and those of your family

and am confident that the _____ Personal Pension is a preferable pension arrangement having regard to your personal position.

My commission / bonus / earnings in the first year from this sale will be £ _____ and in subsequent years will be £ _____ pa.

SIGNED _____

[personal pension provider/intermediary/tied agent]

DATED

24

REGULATION

Introduction

There's a lot of money in pension schemes, so it's not surprising that it's so well regulated. (Some would say that it's not well regulated but over-regulated). Since the value of their pension is worth more than their home to most people, it is probably just as well that there is some kind of supervision.

THE SUPERVISORS

- The **IRSPSS** (Inland Revenue Savings Pensions and Share Schemes Office) of the Inland Revenue check that there is not too much money in a scheme, since they give tax relief.

- The **OPRA** (Occupational Pensions Regulatory Authority) is a 'quango' (semi-independent of government) and checks that schemes comply with the administrative requirements of the law.

- The **National Insurance Contributions Office** checks that there is enough money in the scheme, where it is contracted-out, to meet state pension benefits.

- The **Pensions Ombudsman** acts like a pensions court, where individual members, trustees and others can have their complaints listened to.

- The **Pensions Registry** maintains a register of all schemes, so that people who have lost track of their schemes can try to find where they have gone to.

- The **Pensions Compensation Board** pays out benefits where schemes have lost their funds due to fraud.

- **OPAS** (the Office of the Pensions Advisory Service) is an advisory service to help people with preliminary queries.

- The **DWP** sets out policy in pensions issues, and regulates OPRA and the Pensions Ombudsman.

Each of these bodies is now examined in more detail.

OPRA

The Occupational Pensions Regulatory Authority is supposed to:

- police the trustees, managers and advisers to pension funds

- control the return of surpluses to employers

- receive complaints about the management of schemes ('whistle-blowing')

It can blacklist trustees, fine them, refer serious matters to the courts, and generally interfere as it thinks fit. Fortunately, first indications (it has only been operating since April 1997) are that it will manage with a light touch. And that is just as well, since trustees are not supposed to be professionals.

The National Insurance Contributions Office

The National Insurance Contributions Office is involved where your scheme is 'contracted-out' ie promises to pay some state scheme benefits. It ensures that the proper contributions are made and that there is enough money in the kitty to pay the state-equivalent benefits.

Inland Revenue Savings Pensions and Share Schemes Office

The IRSPSS is the department of the Inland Revenue which deals with occupational pension schemes. Their job is to ensure that the Revenue does not give too much tax relief, that the benefits do not exceed certain levels, and that any surpluses that emerge are dealt with to their advantage.

Their rules are issued in complex memoranda, as well as being set out in statute. They are blessed with a rapidly turning over work force so problems which are put to them are not always answered as promptly as they might be, or with the skill they used to have. There is also a current debate in the industry as to whether their rules are really necessary to protect the interests of the Treasury.

The Pensions Registry

The Pensions Registry (managed by OPRA) is intended to enable people to find out who they left their pension with. With companies being taken over ever more frequently, and changing their name, it can be difficult to remember who employed you twenty years ago.

The Pensions Registry (to which all schemes have to belong) has a computer with the names of schemes and employers to enable people to trace, like squirrels who have lost their nuts, their pension rights.

The Pensions Compensation Board

The Pensions Compensation Board (using money raised by a levy on the industry) pays out benefits which otherwise could not be paid because of fraud in the pension scheme. It does not pay however if the losses are due for example to poor investment or inadequate contributions. It also limits compensation to 90% of the loss.

OPAS

The Office of the Pensions Advisory Service is a government funded advisory service designed to take the steam out of a lot of pensions complaints that are based on inadequate information rather than a genuine grievance.

If they find a serious well-founded complaint, they can try and resolve it amicably – or pass it over to the Ombudsman. They have advisers throughout the country – and best of all are free.

You should have no qualms about referring your members to them, although occasionally some of the advisers get bees in their bonnets about particular issues – and are often seen to be employee rather than employer biased, which is probably not true.

The Pensions Ombudsman

The Pensions Ombudsman, described in more detail below (under Disputes) is a kind of specialist court designed to solve pensions disputes. He has a small office in London and normally hears cases by post. The idea is that he is much cheaper than going to court. But the procedures are still not settled – and sometimes other ombudsmen or courts feel they should control the case.

The DWP

The DWP manages mostly the state scheme; it has obligations in respect of contracted-out rights of personal and occupational schemes, and there are sometimes policy implications for the DSS where company schemes are faced with equal treatment problems, for example.

Investments

Investments are supervised by a wide range of institutions, including the Department of Trade and Industry, the Securities and Investments Board, the Investment Managers Regulatory Organisation, the Personal Investments Authority, and others. The fact that there is regulation and supervision is no guarantee that everything is in order: it is still possible, despite the substantial regulatory framework put in place over the last few years, for funds to disappear. You cannot hope to ensure that fraud or mismanagement will never hit your funds; but you can institute certain checks and balances to limit the risks – diversification, regular reporting and occasional investigations.

25

DISPUTES

> Old communist methods played their part in ensuring Mr Kravchuk's election – above all, the state control of radio, television and many of the newspapers. 'It has been a very unequal campaign,' the main opposition candidate, Vyacheslav Chornovil, told me, 'On television, for instance, we have calculated that Kravchuk received 62 per cent of the coverage of all six candidates. In the Donbass (the coal and steel region of the south-east) I found that many government-run institutions were being used to campaign for Kravchuk – not just the local newspapers, but the post-office as well.' That other powerful mass-medium, rumour, was also being used on Kravchuks' behalf: rumour had it, for example, that Mr Chornovil would take away the farm-workers' pensions when he privatised the collective farms. For me, having heard precisely the same sort of rumours during the Rumanian elections last year being put about by so-called 'ex-communists', there was a strange sense of *déjà entendu*.
>
> *Noel Malcolm, Brave New Nation, Same Old Rulers,*
> *Spectator, 7 December 1991*

Introduction

Even the best-run pension fund, from time to time, becomes involved in a dispute of one kind or another. The trick is in managing the dispute so as to minimise the legal costs and ill-will that can emerge.

Most disputes can be resolved by negotiation – and good communication can often prevent them arising in the first place. In other cases the litigation (ie court fight) is a formal affair: going through the motions to make sure no-one feels aggrieved.

DISPUTE RESOLUTION

- Negotiation
- Internal dispute
- Conciliation
- Pensions Ombudsman
- County Court
- Court of Appeal
- European Court of Justice
- Occupational Pension Regulatory Authority
- Alternative dispute resolution
- OPAS
- Employment tribunal
- High Court
- House of Lords
- Financial Services Authority

If all else fails, many trust deeds make provision for arbitration, and increasingly frequently these days, alternative dispute resolution. The benefit of arbitration is that it is private – but it can cost as much if not more than ordinary litigation. Alternative dispute resolution (ADR) is a method under which an independent person attempts to reconcile the parties. The advantage is that it is cheap, quick and simple, but it doesn't suit everyone – and there is a shortage of people able to carry out the procedure.

Otherwise, the courts can become involved: these include the industrial tribunals, the County Court, the High Court, and others set out in the table. And more recently there is the Pensions Ombudsman – as well as several other ombudsmen.

Internal dispute resolution

It's no fun having a fight with your members – after all, you are there to protect their interests. As before, sometimes the fight is a formal one, to have the matter settled by an outside person so that no-one can afterwards complain. But most complaints are pretty straightforward, and the law now requires trustees to ensure that there is an internal complaints procedure. The procedure can be a simple one: first complaint to be made to, say, the scheme manager or administrator, and if the member is not satisfied then a further complaint to be made to, say, the chairman of the trustees. Only after that should complaints go to say OPAS (Occupational Pensions Advisory Service) or the Pensions Ombudsman.

The Pensions Ombudsman

David Laverick
The Pensions Ombudsman

The Pensions Ombudsman's job is to sort out 'maladministration' in pension schemes, especially those that cannot be resolved either by internal dispute resolution, or by OPAS (see previous Chapter). Anyone can complain, and the costs are at his discretion, but they are likely to be low. There is also no need for a hearing – it can all be done by post. There has been some criticism recently of the Ombudsman's tendency to 'fine' trustees and others for maladministration, but in most cases such fines are usually payable by the fund, and in any event are likely to diminish in frequency.

It is, unfortunately, not the place to go to sort out trustees' problems; his interest is most keenly on the problems of private individuals.

You might like to write for a copy of his last annual report, which sets out a series of common complaints, and which indicate the kinds of weaknesses that schemes are subject to. He may (and does) refuse to accept cases because they are too old, or would be better dealt with elsewhere, or because he doesn't understand them. The big difference between the Pensions Ombudsman and all the other ombudsmen that are around is that he has the powers of a court of law.

The courts

The courts are not the best people to sort out your problems. So far as pensions are concerned, they have the following drawbacks:

Employment tribunals, which can only award judgments up to around £11,000, mostly are involved with contracts of employment (not affecting pension funds directly) although they can interfere and decide whether a contracting-out certificate should be granted despite union objections. They can be categorised as well-meaning but unskilled.

County Courts are involved with disputes up to £50,000, and do have control over pension funds, in theory, in matters up to that amount, or where the trustees or others fail to give information to members or others, or to enforce the Ombudsman's decisions. In practice they are very inexperienced in pensions claims, and could take many (expensive) days to come to a decision.

The *High Court* covers all other matters. Normally pensions cases are dealt with by the Chancery Division of the High Court, the division of the High Court that so upset Dickens in Bleak House. It is a little better nowadays, but not much. In one recent case, the legal fees amounted to £1.5M – after which it was discovered the matter in dispute was £100,000. No-one thought to sack the judge.

Most matters can go to appeal. From an industrial tribunal, appeal is to the Employment Appeal Tribunal (a division of the High Court). From the County Court and High Court you appeal to the Court of Appeal, and then, if still solvent, to the House of Lords. At any time, matters can be referred by a UK court to the European Court of Justice for an opinion on a matter of principle.

Costs The costs of going to court are frightening. It is not the fault of the lawyers – but of the judges, who insist on the production of huge quantities of information, copies of documents of every description and amount, and run a Rolls Royce system of Justice when most would be content with a Ford. The Pensions Ombudsman was designed to cut a swathe through this – however, in many cases the ombudsman system has added to the complexity and length of proceedings, rather than operating (as was intended) as a form of palm-tree justice.

Disputes with the employer

No one likes to fall out with the boss – but as a trustee of a pension fund that very rarely might be your function. The most common problems include failure to pay contributions –or a requirement to return some surplus in the fund.

The best route for everyone is to obtain independent advice, both legal and, where necessary, actuarial.

Only in the ultimate will you need to go to court to have a problem settled. It is unpopular because it is slow, expensive and unpredictable. (You might, in some cases, be able to go to the OPRA or the Ombudsman). Whatever happens, you should make sure that you get your expenses paid for first – either you will have power to reclaim your costs in the deed – or you may need to go to the court first to get your costs approved out of the fund under the 'Rule in Beddoes case' in case your lawyer has overlooked it.

PART III

THE BLUFFER'S GUIDE

APPENDIX I

THE BLUFFER'S GUIDE

When pensions people get together for a party, one of the party games they play is 'Definitions and Abbreviations' – there are not many who can score 100%. Set out below are some of the terms used in this Handbook, and others which you may come across in practice.

Accrual is the system under which benefits are earned year-by-year in a pension scheme. The more years you work, the more rights you accrue (or earn, perhaps). It is important in pensions at the moment because it is the basis of the argument the UK Government is using in the European Court to explain that pension rights in the UK do not magically appear once you reach retirement age, but are painfully acquired (and funded for) year-by-year.

Actuary is a mathematician who by definition always gets it wrong. He estimates what he thinks the funds will earn over the next twenty years or so, what your salary will be over the next thirty years, and on the basis of these and other assumptions, calculates backwards how much money needs to be put in the kitty now. Even though he can predict the future no better than an astrologer (according to one blessed judge) he is worth every penny of his substantial fees.

Additional Voluntary Contribution is the extra contribution (not more than 15% of salary) which a member can pay into a scheme to buy extra benefits. Members now have a right to make such contributions – if they do not bump up against Inland Revenue limits.

Administrator is an Inland Revenue technical term to describe the person with whom the buck stops as far as they are concerned. It is your job to ensure that is not you – and is someone like the pensions manager or insurance company.

Appropriate personal pension is a **personal pension** which provides for an employed person a SERPS benefit through a personal arrangement with a bank, building society, insurance company or unit trust. Because of the immense costs of administration charged by insurers and others – and it is not guaranteed – it is peculiarly inappropriate for most people, hence its name.

Beauty Parade is a competition you can hold where you invite potential advisers to display themselves to best advantage, indicate how little they charge, and how special is their service. It can be by post, or you can actually meet a short list. They can involve huge expense for the contestants, and are surprisingly time-consuming and exhausting to judge. You should not normally kiss the winner.

Contracting-in is the opposite of **contracting-out**.

Contracting-out is a system under which a company pension scheme provides benefits equivalent to one of the state pensions (formerly the State Earnings Related Pension Scheme (SERPS), now the State Second Pension (S2P)) in exchange for the employer and employee enjoying reduced national insurance contributions. In recent years, the government offered a bribe (incentive) to persuade people to contract-out and anticipated the cost would be about £750M – it actually cost around £8B, say 2p on the income tax.

Corporate Trustee is simply a trustee who is a limited company, rather than an individual.

Customer Agreement is an agreement between the trustees and the investment managers, which is required by law. Although it must state certain terms, the content of those terms is open to negotiation. Most customer agreements are very user-unfriendly.

Deferred Pensioners are people who have left the company usually to go and get a better, higher-paid job with a competitor. You may feel that they have forfeited your sympathy, but they are nonetheless beneficiaries under the scheme, and you must treat them in the same manner as you treat other beneficiaries.

Derivatives are so-called investments which are one stage removed from reality. For example, instead of buying *a share in Marks and Spencer*, you might buy *the right to buy a share in Marks and Spencer in three months time at a price fixed now* and hope that the price will rise in the meantime. If the price falls you will still have to buy the share at a loss, with money you might not have at the time. For most pension funds they are not suitable, unless used in conjunction with some other strategy, such as the intention to buy an investment overseas. Take great care and special advice. Derivatives include Swaps, Futures and Options – they are not explained because you should keep away from them.

Independent Trustees are trustees who are not connected with the employer or the fund's advisers. They are increasingly common these days to help trustees avoid any pressures arising from conflicts of interest.

Personal Pension is a pension which operates like a money-box for an individual. He or she saves money each month and hopes that when retirement is reached it will be enough to buy a reasonable pension after the investment management charges, dealing fees, commission expenses, marketing overheads and administration costs have been paid, and that the stock market will not have collapsed three days before retirement. But it can be useful for young, mobile employees.

Preservation is a law which states that you do not forfeit your pension rights just because you leave the employer sometime before retirement. It is not a perfect law, but it is very much better than it used to be, and is getting better all the time. It is explained in Chapter 18.

Protected Rights are the rights which, in a **contracted-out money purchase scheme,** replace the rights you would have earned under SERPS. Since they are money-purchase, you have no idea what they are until retirement, so that they are not in fact protected at all.

Requisite Benefits are the benefits that a **contracted-out** scheme must offer to be allowed to contract-out.

S2P is the State Second Pension which was introduced in 2002 to replace over time the State Earnings Related Pension (SERPS). It is a flat rate pension which gives pensions to people who are earning under £10,800 (2002/3) as though they had been earning that amount. Common sense dictates that since it is a flat rate pension it will eventually be merged with the Basic State Pension.

Soft Commission is so called because trustees who are soft-hearted allow fund managers to enjoy what is in effect Christmas twice-a-year. It allows investment managers to use stockbrokers to buy and sell your shares at a high commission rate so that the stockbrokers can buy them gifts (not normally cheapies, like silk stockings and champagne, but really expensive ones like Reuters screens). Don't allow it without good cause. The Myners Review published by the Treasury in March 2001 recommended the abolition of soft commission arrangements.

Split Fund is an arrangement which means that you divide the assets of your scheme between different fund managers and watch them compete. Some schemes have up to a dozen fund managers, but even for the smaller schemes a couple is not a bad idea.

Survivors is the modern term for 'widows and widowers'; it is shorter and discrimination-free.

Abbreviations

AVC Additional Voluntary Contribution (see Definitions)

COMPS, CIMPS, COSRS, CISRS, COMBS etc Contracted-out Money Purchase Schemes, Contracted-in Money Purchase Schemes, Contracted-out Salary Related Schemes, Contracted-in Salary Related Schemes, Contracted-out Mixed Benefit Schemes.

DWP The Department of Work and Pensions, which governs contracting-out, pensions' policy and state pensions.

GMP's Guaranteed Minimum Pension being the replacement (by the company scheme) for the state second tier pension. Nowadays, it may not be guaranteed or provide a minimum.

IRNICO Inland Revenue National Insurance Contributions Office, responsible for, amongst other things, supervising contracting-in arrangements.

IRSPSS Inland Revenue Savings Pensions and Share Schemes Office.

MFR Minimum Funding Requirement – the minimum amount of assets you must have in a final salary type scheme. The idea was to ensure that if the employer went bust, there would be enough to pay benefits; in fact the requirement is much more modest.

MNT/MND Member Nominated Trustee/Director – a trustee nominated by the membership.

OPRA The Occupational Pensions Regulatory Authority.

APPENDIX II

THE BRITISH PENSION SYSTEM

"Ministers, he [Sir Michael Partridge, Permanent Secretary at the Department of Social Security] said, regarded the far greater take-up of the scheme – and thus its far higher cost – as a "success", not a matter for apology.

But he also disclosed that the cost of [contracting-out] rebates had been so high that ministers had had to transfer three benefits, including statutory maternity and sick pay, out of national insurance and onto general taxation, in order to balance the National Insurance Fund's books. Michael Latham, Tory MP for Rutland and Melton told Sir Michael: "Any more successes [like that] and we are all ruined."

Nicholas Timmins, The Independent, 18 December 1990

The System

The British pensions system appeals particularly to people who like to do the Times crossword puzzle. It is one of the most complicated and over-regulated in the world and there are relatively few who fully understand all its implications. In brief, it works as follows:

- Everyone who has a job, including the self-employed, and earns over around £5,000 pa is entitled to a *basic state pension*, provided sufficient contributions have been paid over the years.

- In addition, an *additional state pension*, the State Second Pension (which replaces the former SERPS, State Earnings Related Pension Scheme) is payable to employed people; those who have not been employed are treated as though they had earned £10,800 (2002/03). This does not apply to the self-employed. This pension can be paid either by the state (when it is said to be contracted-in) or by an employer's pension scheme (when it is said to be contracted-out).

- In addition, around 10 million people are earning rights under a company or *occupational pension*. The rules vary tremendously from scheme to scheme, but the Inland Revenue set down either maximum contributions (in a money purchase scheme) or maximum benefits (in a final salary scheme).

- Some people have decided not to join their company scheme. They can do nothing – or make contributions to a *personal pension scheme*. A personal pension is the only kind of pension which self-employed can enjoy. A personal pension can only be money purchase, not final salary.

The Revenue Rules

The Inland Revenue (Inland Revenue Savings Pensions and Share Schemes Office) lays down the rules which decide whether pension funds are eligible for tax relief. Their jurisdiction, nowadays, is diminishing slightly as they have foregone control of unapproved, unfunded schemes which provide pensions for top-earners; but in most cases they are concerned to police schemes to ensure that the benefits they pay are within bounds. They control benefits (in final salary schemes – in money purchase schemes they control contributions) so that the state does not give away too much tax relief.

It is not clear whether the skies would fall in if the IRSPSS were abolished, and control was simply on the benefits payable in simple terms; but the controls that have been imposed by the IRSPSS on benefits are so abstruse that they can no longer be policed properly by them. There are around eight different tax systems that can apply to pensions, depending on when the member joined, when the scheme was set up, and what kind of scheme it is.

Nonetheless, the IRSPSS police all changes to the rules, and check employer sponsorship carefully. Your advisers and pension fund manager are in awe of the Revenue and very properly so too; their livelihoods are at stake if they are crossed. The Revenue rule by discretion rather than statute, so they can make up their minds as they go along.

Self-Administered and Insured

All company pension schemes in the UK are, strictly speaking, self-administered, ie managed by trustees. But schemes which have delegated all the investment and administration to insurance companies are said to be 'insured'.

For trustees, there may be problems with insured schemes. First, it is sometimes very difficult to work out what the management and investment expenses are (usually higher than self-administered schemes for all but the smallest funds). Secondly, the actuary sometimes has a conflict of interest between acting for you and acting for his employer (the insurance company), and may be tempted to suggest higher contribution rates, for example, than might be strictly necessary (in order to raise fees) or lower amounts than might be prudent (in order to get business). Thirdly, the contracts imposed by insurers (if you ever get a chance to see them) can be rather one-sided – in their favour – with unacceptable penalty clauses for early discontinuance. Which is why almost all the larger pension schemes tend to go self-administered as soon as they are old enough.

Money Purchase and Final Salary

A final salary scheme is one of the great antidotes to the effect of inflation on pensioners, although it is not perfect. It promises benefits related to the salary at the date of leaving, usually according to some formula related to the number of years you have worked with the company. One example is to promise a pension of 1/60th of final salary for each year you work with the company. If you work for 40 years, you will get 40/60ths, ie 2/3rds. With luck there may be some element of inflation protection once the pension starts in payment. (The Americans call this kind of scheme 'benefits-related').

A money purchase scheme doesn't promise anything at all. It establishes a kind of piggy-bank into which your contributions and those of the employer (if any) are paid. The money is invested – and at the end of the day whatever is available is gambled with an insurance company. Your bet is that you will live a long time, and the premium or wager will pay off. The insurance company hopes on the other hand you will die soon, so it can make a profit. The value of the pension depends not on your salary at retirement, but on what the accumulated pot will buy at the time – and the value of the pot may be affected by changes in the value of the shares or other assets at the date you retire.

Unfunded Schemes

The point of a funded scheme is that if the employer does not meet his promise for any reason (eg bankruptcy) there will be money available to meet the promise. The Inland Revenue does not allow, however, (with some exceptions), funding of pension schemes in relation to higher salaries (at the time of writing £97,200), so there is no security for those higher pensions. In addition there is no law in the UK which requires adequate funds to be in the kitty to meet the pensions expectations (unlike eg Ireland).

AVC's

Because very few people actually spend 40 years with one company, very few people actually accrue full pension benefits (for why not, see Chapter 18). They are therefore allowed to make additional contributions (within limits – 15% of their salary) to their scheme. These are known as Additional Voluntary Contributions, for obvious reasons.

If they are made outside the pension scheme, they are called Free-Standing AVC's. The Inland Revenue is paranoid that in some cases the amount of contributions will allow you to draw a pension in excess of their limits, and an immense bureaucratic structure has been imposed to make sure this can never happen.

APPENDIX III

PENSIONS IN PICTURES

Pensions and Taxation

Relief for	£ million
Employee contributions to occupational pension schemes[1,2]	4,000
Investment income of occupational pension schemes[1,3]	3,200
Lump sum payments to pensioners[1]	1,400
Contributions to personal pensions (including retirement annuity premia and FSAVC's	3,300

1 The total cost of tax reliefs for occupational pension schemes cannot be calculated by adding together the cost of individual reliefs as this would imply a considerable degree of multiple taxation.

2 It is not possible to provide a reliable breakdown of the total cost of relief between basic rate and higher rate taxpayers.

3 Assuming tax relief at the basic rate of income tax.

4 Including income tax relief on employers' contributions to personal pensions on the basis that, under present arrangements, employers' contributions are not taxable as a benefit in kind of the employee.

5 It is not possible to provide reliable estimates of the cost of exemption for investment income and lump sum payments related to retirement annuity contracts and personal pensions.

Source: Inland Revenue Statistics, Table T7.9 2002.

Basic State Pension

Since 1948, single person, pa

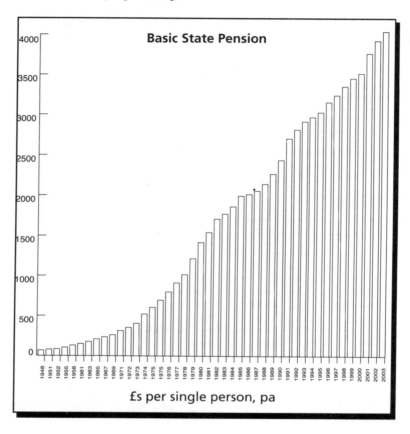

£s per single person, pa

Future Cost of State Pensions

The Government is concerned about the future cost of state pensions, which is why it encourages private pension provision with tax breaks.

Occupational Pensions as Part of Income

The average pensioner's total net income increased by over 33% in real terms between 1979 and 1988. Table 1 below shows a breakdown of the individual components which contributed towards this increase.

TABLE 1

Pensioners Incomes	1974	1979	1988	Real terms increase 1974-9	Real terms increase 1979-88
Total SS bens	47.20	53.00	60.70	12%	14%
Occ Pensions	12.40	13.90	27.70	12%	99%
Savings income	11.30	9.50	20.00	-16%	110%
Earnings	14.30	10.40	9.80	-27%	-6%
Total Gross inc	85.10	86.90	118.20	2%	36%
Total Net inc	77.40	79.60	106.30	3%	33%

1   Source: Family Expenditure Survey

2   £s per week at 1988 prices

In 1988 74% of all pensioners received income from savings and the average amount that they received was £29.80. Also, 51% of all pensioners had an occupational pension and the average amount received was £47.00. Table 2 on the next page shows the comparable figures for 1974 and 1979.

TABLE 2

Pensioners income from savings and occupational pensions 1974, 1979 and 1988

	1974	1979	1988
% of pensioners with savings income	53	62	74
Average amount (per week) received from savings income	£21.50	£15.30	£29.80
% of pensioners with occupational pensions	35	41	51
Average amount (per week) received from occupational pension	£33.40	£33.70	£47.00

1   Source: Family Expenditure Survey

2   £s per week at 1988 prices

3   Averages are based on those pensioners who actually received savings income or occupational pensions

A greater proportion of those pensioners who had retired only recently, ie within the five years immediately preceding the survey, received incomes from these sources. In 1988, 78% of the recently retired pensioners had savings income while 63% received income from an occupational pension.

In 1988 20% of all pensioners' savings income was derived from 'non-bank' sources, eg from share dividends; the same was true of 14% of savings income in 1979.

Other points to emerge from the analysis are:

- the proportion of pensioners in the lowest quintile of income distribution was 28% in 1988 compared with around 40% in 1979

- single pensioners who receive all their income from state benefits have income 25% higher in real terms than those in 1979; the increase for married couples was 22%.

- the average pensioners gross income represented 59% of the average earnings of all manual workers

- 46% of pensioners owned their homes outright in 1988 compared with only 38% in 1979.

Source: DSS Press Release 23 July 1991.

Investment Performance: How well did it do?

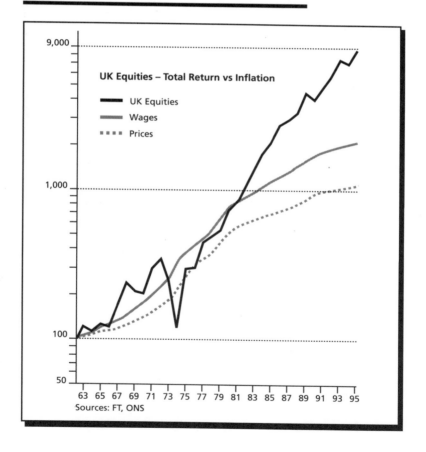

Pension Fund Assets: International Comparisons

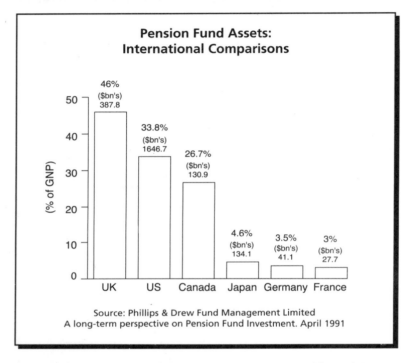

The amounts in pension funds are sometimes treated by politicians as disposable capital. The sums involved are considerable.

Source: E P Davis, The Development of Pension Funds, an international comparison, [1991] Bank of England Quarterly 380

Pension As a Personal Asset

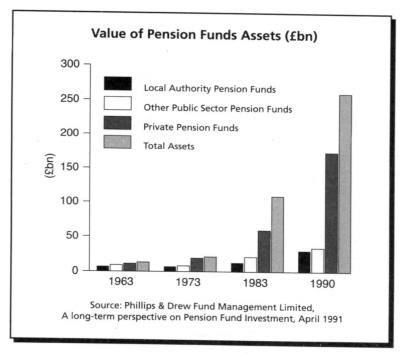

Value of Pension Funds Assets (£bn)

Source: Phillips & Drew Fund Management Limited,
A long-term perspective on Pension Fund Investment, April 1991

Pensions are becoming more important in relation to other assets for retired people.

Source: E P Davis, The Development of Pension Funds, an international comparison, [1991] Bank of England Quarterly 380

Support Ratios

The support ratio is the number of pensioners and other dependants (such as children, unemployed, students) compared with the number of workers. If the birth rate declines, there are fewer workers to support more dependants. The position in the UK is not as bad as some of our competitors, especially Japan.

Number of people of working age per pensioner: the support ratio				
	1990	2010	2030	2050
People of working age per pensioner	3.4	3.1	2.4	2.6

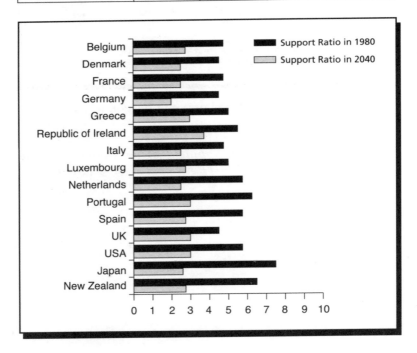

Wrinklies: In the UK

The increasing number of older people is a cause of concern to state pensions planners.

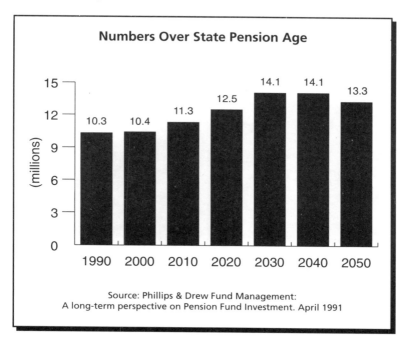

Numbers Over State Pension Age

Source: Phillips & Drew Fund Management:
A long-term perspective on Pension Fund Investment. April 1991

Wrinklies: International Comparisons

An alternative way of looking at the problem is to look at the change over the next 30 years:

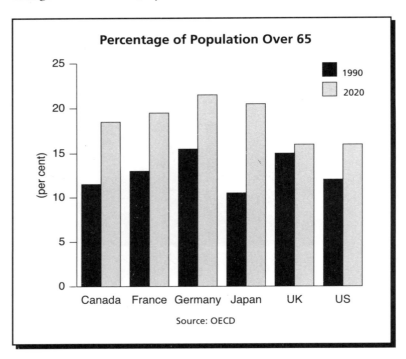

Inflation: The Value of a £

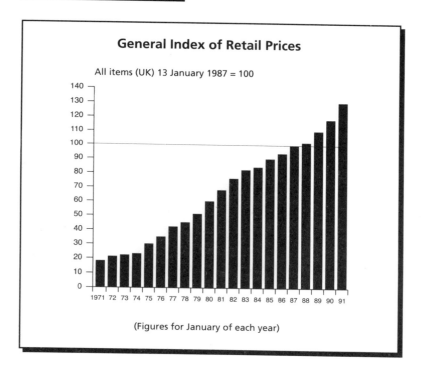

General Index of Retail Prices

All items (UK) 13 January 1987 = 100

(Figures for January of each year)

Life Expectancy: How Long Will You Live?

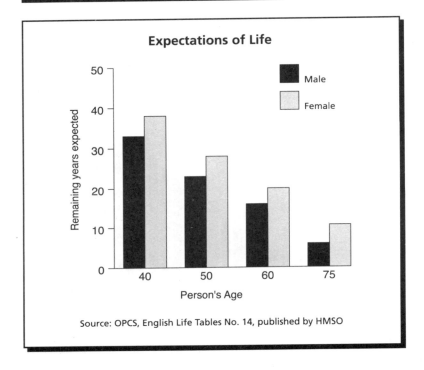

Source: OPCS, English Life Tables No. 14, published by HMSO

APPENDIX IV

BLUFFERS' CASES

One of the things that irritates many trustees is the throwaway reference made in conversation by advisers to famous law cases. Set down below are brief outlines of some of the more important cases, and ones which are referred to frequently in practice. Because three of the cases deal with the Imperial Group pension scheme, they have been given their alternative colloquial names to avoid confusion. References are given to enable further study, if required.

Investments

Scargill

Arthur Scargill, the miners' leader, was a trustee with other union members of the mineworkers' pension scheme. When the in-house fund managers produced an investment plan and sought the approval of the trustees, he objected. The plan included investments in property in the United States, and in oil shares; the union objected on the grounds that a UK fund should invest in the UK to support the UK economy, and that a coal pension fund should not support the shares of a competing fuel industry.

The judge held that the only objective which trustees should bear in mind is the financial performance of the fund; trustees should not promote their external objectives which might have an adverse impact on the fund's performance. It did not hold that social and ethical investments were inappropriate for pension funds; but, where these criteria are involved, trustees need to ensure that their members will not suffer. (Cowan v Scargill, Re Mineworkers' Pension Scheme Trusts [1985] Ch 270)

Grumman

This is an American case – but very relevant to current problems. Although it is forbidden for pension funds to buy too much of its parent company's shares nowadays, it may have some shares, or shares in the predator. Should it take the best price – or help out the employer? Conventional trustee thinking should say: take the money and run. But other minds have thought that you could take into account job prospects and other matters affecting the members for whom you care.

The Department of Labor in the States (which looks after pension schemes) sued the trustees who had refused to sell the Grumman fund's shares in Grumman, the fighter aircraft manufacturer, to Lockheed which had made a juicy offer. But by the time the case came to trial, the share price was higher than ever, so the Department could not show the trustees had made a loss, and dropped the case. (Blankenship v Boyle (1971) 329 F Supp 1089)

Surpluses – Whose Money is it?

Hillsdown 1

When Hillsdown bought a subsidiary company from the Imperial Group, the bulk transfer payment, received in respect of the members who became employed by Hillsdown, did not include a share of the surplus in the Imperial fund. The judge said that in reality the surplus was 'temporary surplus funding' by the employer, and that in this particular case the members had no interest in it. For a short time it indicated that there was nothing wrong in employers claiming a return of surplus. (Re Imperial Foods Ltd Pension Scheme [1986] 1 WLR 717).

Courage

The next year, in a case involving the same scheme, a different judge held, however, that surpluses could not be automatically recovered by an employer as part of a commercial transaction.

There was no principle that a surplus, by its nature, was the employer's, even in a 'balance-of-cost' scheme – that is where the employer pays whatever contributions are deemed necessary by an actuary. This made it difficult for advisers to determine when a surplus could be recaptured by employers, and when it could not. (Ryan v Imperial Brewing and Leisure, Re Courage Group's Pension Schemes [1987] 1 WLR 495)

Mettoy

When the Corgi toy car company went bust, it left behind a string of debts and a large pension scheme. The scheme was so large it had around £9M surplus, left after the scheme trustees had bought the appropriate benefits for all the pensioners and other members. The question was whether the liquidator of the company could also act as trustee of the fund, and pay himself (as liquidator) the surplus, which he could then pass on to the creditors of the company.

After a fair chunk of the surplus had been spent on legal fees (not just the fault of the lawyers – the judge insists on all conceivable parties (such as widows and children) being separately represented) and many years travelling through the courts, the judge simply said that he would approve a deal involving improvement of benefits and return of surplus, if it were brought to him. At the time of writing, it is understood the case is going to appeal. (Re Mettoy Pension Scheme [1990] Pensions Law Reports 9)

Davis v Richards and Wallington

This is another case where the employer was in liquidation. The judge said that if it had not been for the fact that the documentation was in force, the surplus in relation to the employers' contributions could be returned to the employer – and the surplus in relation to the employees' contributions would have to go to the Crown! The judgment seems deeply flawed, but it shows that there are several ways of looking at what a surplus is.

Fisons

Fisons, the fertiliser and chemicals company, sold its agrochemicals subsidiary to a another company. In the time between the sale and the time when the bulk transfer payment was made, in respect of the employees who had transferred, the stock market rose. Should the transfer value reflect that a surplus had arisen – or be based on the original deal set out in the sale and purchase agreement? In yet another rather odd judgment the Court of Appeal said that where the employees stay in the scheme while the new employer sets up a new scheme, they are entitled to a share of the surplus. The case is a worry for trustees, and they need to ensure that their lawyers have covered the position in the sale and purchase agreement. (Stannard v Fisons Trust Ltd [1992] 1RLR 227).

Hillsdown 2

In a later case, involving a different surplus, Hillsdown was ordered to return a substantial surplus to a scheme which had been repatriated to the employer. The case was based on technicalities, and in future, since all applications for return of surplus must be approved by OPRA, it is unlikely that the courts would order such a return – especially since it does nothing to benefit the members, but just sits in the scheme. (Re Imperial Foods Pension Scheme [1986] 1WLR 717).

Equal Treatment

Barber

Mr Barber was made redundant at the age of 52 and his employer offered people within ten years of retirement an early retirement pension. His normal retirement age was 65, and he was therefore not within 10 years – but a female colleague in the same position but whose retirement age was 60 (reflecting the state retirement age) would have been entitled to call for an early retirement pension.

The European Court of Justice held that pensions were to be regarded as pay, covered by the equal pay law of the Treaty of Rome, and Mr Barber (or rather his widow – he had died by the time the case came to court) was entitled to the benefit.

The major problem was whether the decision affected pension rights acquired by men before the date of the judgment (May 1990) – if so it would have enabled all men to have an unreduced early retirement pension, cost UK plc around £50B, and bankrupted a number of employers. Fortunately, before any further cases went to court the matter was settled by an amendment to the Treaty of Rome, which indicated that pension rights earned before May 1990 were not covered. (Barber v Guardian Royal Exchange Assurance Group, Case C262/88, [1990] 2 All ER 660)

Employers and Trustees

Mihlenstedt

A bank clerk in her thirties complained of illness and asked for an ill-health early retirement pension. Because such a pension is very expensive to provide the trustees could only give it with the consent of the employer. Since medical examinations failed to disclose any illness, the employer refused. The judge said that the employer's refusal had to be fair (and as though he were a trustee of the scheme) and not just based on a desire to save money for the company. In fact, the company had behaved properly – but the case imposed a new obligation on employers, and made the use of employer's vetoes problematical. The case is a problem for employers, rather than trustees. (Mihlenstedt v Barclays Bank International Ltd [1989] Pensions Law Reports 124)

Imperial

The employer tried to squeeze surplus out of a (closed) pension scheme by saying that he would not agree to any increases in pensions-in-payment over 5% (on which he had a veto) unless the trustees and members agreed to move over to another pension scheme. The judge said that employers had to use such vetoes (consents) as though they were trustees, not to force through decisions under which they could benefit. Since the company was Hanson, which had a reputation for attempting to squeeze pension funds, there was not much sympathy for the employer. But the decision raises the interesting question of what is the function of such a veto, if it is not to save the company money. (Imperial Group Pension Trust Ltd v Imperial Tobacco Ltd)

APPENDIX V

ADDRESSES

Trustees can usually rely on their in-house support (if any) or their advisers to deal on a day-to-day basis with the regulators and other institutions. But there may be times when you need to get in touch direct, perhaps to check that something has been done, or to complain about the quality of service of an adviser. Set out below are some of the more useful addresses and phone numbers.

ACCOUNTS

Pensions Research Accountants Group (PRAG)
c/o Merchant Navy Pensions Administration Limited
Ashcombe House, The Crescent, Leatherhead
Surrey KT22 8LQ
01372 386000 • www.prag.org.uk

Accounting Standards Board
Holborn Hall, 100 Gray's Inn Road
London WC1X 8AL
020 7404 8818 • www.asb.org.uk

Association of Certified Chartered Accounts (ACCA)
29 Lincoln's Inn Fields
London WC2A 3EE
020 7396 7000 • www.acca.co.uk

Chartered Institute of Management Accountants (CIMA)
The Registry, 63 Portland Place
London W1N 4AB
020 7637 2311 • www.cima.org.uk

Chartered Institute of Public Finance and Accountancy
3 Robert Street
London WC2N 6RL
020 7543 5600 • www.cipfa.org.uk

Financial Reporting Council www.frc.org.uk
Holborn Hall, 100 Gray's Inn Road
London WC1X 8AL
020 7611 9700

Institute of Chartered Accountants in England and Wales
Chartered Accountants Hall, PO Box 433
London EC2P 2BJ
020 7920 8100 • www.icaew.co.uk

Institute of Chartered Accountants of Scotland
CA House, 21 Haymarket Yard
Edinburgh EH12 5BH
0131 347 0100 • www.icas.org.uk

ACTUARIAL MATTERS

In England and Wales:
Institute of Actuaries
Staple Inn Hall,High Holborn
London WC1V 7QJ
020 7632 2100 • www.actuaries.org .uk

Consulting Actuaries:
Association of Consulting Actuaries
No.1 Wardrobe Place
London EC4V 5AG
020 7248 8265 • Fax: 020 7236 1889 • www.aca.org.uk

In Scotland:

Faculty of Actuaries in Scotland
Maclaurin House, 18 Dublin Street
Edinburgh EH1 3PP
0131 240 1300 • www.actuaries.org.uk

Government Actuary's Department
New King's Beam House, 22 Upper Ground
London SE1 9RJ
020 7211 2600 • www.gad.gov.uk

ADMINISTRATION

Institute of Chartered Secretaries and Administrators
16 Park Crescent
London W1B 1AH
020 7580 4741 • www.icsa.org.uk

CONSULTANTS

Society of Pensions Consultants
The Society of Pension Consultants
St Bartholomew House, 92 Fleet Street
London EC4Y 1DG
020 7353 1688 • www.spc.uk.com

CONSUMER AFFAIRS

Complaints and Remedies:
Office of Pensions Advisory Service
11 Belgrave Road
London SW1V 1RB
Helpline 0845-6012923 • www.opas.org.uk

Occupational Schemes:
Pensions Ombudsman
11 Belgrave Road
London SW1V 1RB
020 7834 9144 • www.pensions-ombudsman.org.uk

Personal Pensions:
Financial Ombudsman Service
Financial Ombudsman Service, South Quay Plaza, 183 Marsh Wall
London E14 9SR
020 7964 1000 • www.financial-ombudsman.org.uk

Supervision:
Occupational Pensions Regulatory Authority
Invicta House, Trafalgar Place
Brighton BN1 4DW
01273 627600 • www.opra.gov.uk

EMPLOYERS

Institute of Directors
116 Pall Mall
London SW1 5ED
020 7839 1233 • www.iod.com

Chartered Management Institute
2 Savoy Court Strand
London WC2R 0EZ
020 7497 0580 • Fax: +44 (0)20 7497 0463 • www.inst-mgt.org.uk

Chartered Institute of Personnel and Development
CIPD House, Camp Road, Wimbledon
London SW19 4UX
020 8971 9000 • Fax 020 8263 3333 • www.cipd.org.uk

EUROPE AND INTERNATIONAL

The Double Century Club
Sheila Nettleton, 19 Langham Court
Wyke Road, West Wimbledon
London SW20 8RP
020 8946 3597 • dspace.dial.pipex.com/town/walk/gmf93/dcc/

European Union (Commission)
Rue de la Loi/Wetstraat 200
B-1049 Brussels
(32-2) 299 11 11
www. europa.eu.int/comm/internal_market/pensions/index_en.htm

The Pension Service (DWP)
International Pension Centre, Tyneview Park
Newcastle upon Tyne NE98 1BA.
0191 218 7777 • www.dwp.gov.uk/www.thepensionservice.gov.uk

FINANCE

Association of Corporate Treasurers
Ocean House, 10/12 Little Trinity Lane
London EC4V 2DJ
020 7213 9728 • www.treasurers.org

INDUSTRY

National Association of Pension Funds
NIOC House, 4 Victoria Street
London SW1H 0NE
020 7808 1300 • www.napf.co.uk

CBI Pensions Working Party
Employment Affairs Directorate
CBI, 103 New Oxford Street
London WC1A 1DU
020 7379 7400 • www.cbi.org.uk

Chartered Insurance Institute
20 Aldermanbury
London EC2V 7HY
020 8989 8464 • www.cii.co.uk

Association of British Insurers
51 Gresham Street
London EC2V 7HQ
020 7600 3333 • www.abi.org.uk

British Insurance Brokers Association
14 Bevis Marks
London EC3A 7NT
020 7623 9043 • www.biba.org.uk

Society of Financial Advisors
20 Aldermanbury
London EC2V 7HY
020 8989 8464 • www.sofa.org

Society of Pensions Consultants
The Society of Pension Consultants
St Bartholomew House, 92 Fleet Street
London EC4Y 1DG
020-7353 1688 • www.spc.uk.com

Local Government Pensions Committee
Layden House, 76-86 Turnmill Street
London EC1M 5QU
020 7296 6781 • www.lg-employers.gov.uk/pensions

Local Government Pension Scheme
Pensions Administration Division, Finance Department
Civic Centre, St Peter's Square, Wolverhampton
West Midlands WV1 1SL
01902 554600 • www.lgps.org.uk

INVESTMENT

Association of Investment Trust Companies
8-13 Chiswell Street
London EC4Y 4YY
020 7282 5555 • www.aitc.co.uk

Investment Management Association
65 Kingsway
London WC2B 6TD
020 7831 0898 • www.investmentfunds.org.uk

British Property Federation
British Property Federation, 7th Floor, 1 Warwick Row
London SW1E 5ER
020 7828 0111 •www.bpf.propertymall.com

British Venture Capital Association
3 Clements Inn
London WC2A 2AZ.
020-7025 2950 • www.bvca.co.uk

Building Societies Association
3 Saville Row
London W1S 3PB
020 7437 0655 • www.bsa.org.uk

Council of Mortgage Lenders
3 Saville Row
London W1S 3PB
020 7437 0075 • www.cml.org.uk

Institute of Investment Professionals
21 Ironmonger Lane
London EC2V 8EY
020 7796 3000 • www.uksip.org

Institutional Shareholders Committee
51 Gresham Street
London EC2V 7HQ
020 7696 8990 • www.abi.org.uk

**London International Financial Futures
and Options Exchange**
Cannon Bridge
London EC4R 3XX
020 7623 0444 • www.liffe.com

London Investment Banking Association
6 Frederick's Place
London EC2R 8BT
020 7796 3606 • www.liba.org.uk

London Stock Exchange
Old Broad Street
London EC2N 1HP
020 7797 1000 • www.londonstockexchange.com

NAPF Investment Committee
NIOC House, 4 Victoria Street
London SW1H 0NE
020 7808 1300 • www.napf.co.uk

ProShare UK Ltd
ProShare (UK) Ltd, Centurion House, 24 Monument St
London EC3R 8AQ
020 7220 1730 • www.proshare.org

Royal Institute of Chartered Surveyors
12 Great George Street
London SW1P 3AD
020 7222 7000 • www.rics.org.uk

LAWYERS

Association of Pension Lawyers
PMI House, 4-10 Artillery Lane
London E1 7LS
0870 240 6036 • www.apl.org.uk

Law Society of England and Wales
113 Chancery Lane
London WC2A 1PL
020 7242 1222 • www.lawsoc.org.uk

Law Society of Scotland
26 Drumsheugh Gardens
Edinburgh EH3 7YR
0131 226 7411 • www.lawscot.org.uk

PERSONAL PENSIONS

Association of British Insurers
51 Gresham Street
London EC2V 7HQ
020 7600 3333 • www.abi.org.uk

POLITICAL

All-party Parliamentary Group on Occupational Pensions
c/o John Butterfield MP, Palace of Westminster
London SW1A OAA
020 7219 3000

War Widows Association
48 Pall Mall
London SW1Y 3JY
0870 2411 305

POPULATION AND DEMOGRAPHY

Government Actuary's Department
New King's Beam House, 22 Upper Ground
London SE1 9RJ
020 7211 2600 • www.gad.gov.uk

Office of National Statistics
1 Drummond Gate
London SW1V 2QQ
020 7233 9233 • www.statistics.gov.uk

PENSIONS PROFESSION

Pension Managers
The Pensions Management Institute
PMI House, 4-10 Artillery Lane
London E1 7LS
020 7247 1452 • www.pensions-pmi.org.uk

REGULATION

Bank of England
Threadneedle Street
London EC2R 8AH
020 7601 4444 • www.bankofengland.co.uk

Department of Work and Pensions
The Adelphi, 1-11 John Adam Street
London WC2N 6HT
020 7962 8000 • www.dwp.gov.uk

Financial Services Authority
25 The North Colonnade, Canary Wharf
London E14 5HS
020 7676 1000 • www.fsa.gov.uk

Inland Revenue National Insurance Contributions Office
Benton Park View
Newcastle upon Tyne NE98 1ZZ
0191 213 5000 • www.inlandrevenue.gov.uk/nic

Inland Revenue, Savings Pensions Share Schemes
New Wing Somerset House
London WC2R 1LB
020 7438 6622 • www.inlandrevenue.gov.uk

Pensions Compensation Board
11 Belgrave Road
London SW1V 1RB
020 7828 9794

Registrar of Pension Schemes
PO Box 1NN
Newcastle on Tyne NE99 1NN
0191 225 6316 • www.opra.gov.uk/registry

SMALL SCHEMES

Schemes with fewer than 12 members, controlling director schemes:

Association of Pensioneer Trustees
Michael Norris, JB Trustees, 20 Bank Street, Lutterworth
Leicester LE17 4AG
01455 559711 • www.pensioneers.org

Self-invested personal pensions:

SIPP Providers Group
Francis Moore, Shortsmead, Alvediston
Salisbury SP5 5LD
01722 781028 • www.sipp-provider-group.org.uk

TAX

The Chartered Institute of Taxation
12 Upper Belgrave Street
London SW1X 8BB
020 7235 9381 • www.tax.org.uk

Inland Revenue Savings Pension Share Schemes Office
Yorke House, PO Box 62, Castle Meadow Road
Nottingham NG2 1BG
0115 974 1600 • www.inlandrevenue.gov.uk

TRUSTEES

Association of Corporate Trustees
The Secretary, 3 Brackerne Close
Cooden, Bexhill-on-Sea
East Sussex TN39 3BT
01424 844144 • www.trustees.org.uk

PMI Trustee Group
Pensions Management Institute, PMI House 4-10 Artillery Lane
London E1 7LS
020 7247 1452 • www.pensions-pmi.org.uk

TUC Member Trustees Network
Trades Union Congress
Congress House, Great Russell Street
London WC1B 3LS
020 7636 4030 • www.tuc.org.uk/pensions

Public Trustee
81 Chancery Lane
London WC2A 1DD
020 7911 7127 • www.offsol.demon.co.uk

APPENDIX VI

FURTHER READING

The library of books and videos on pensions is now almost without number. If you'd like to explore this fascinating subject more clearly, some of the more readable include:

PERIODICALS

There is one 'official' periodical, *Pensions World* (www.pensions world.co.uk). The publishers have not put much money into it in recent years, but it is widely read in the industry, it does have the basic information and a monthly shower of leaflets and booklets, some of which are worth reading – and it is relatively cheap (£95.85). There is a summary of legal developments at the end which is a useful summary.

Most of the others are also designed for pensions technicians or salesmen, but *Occupational Pensions* (http://www.irseclipse. co.uk, £200 pa), designed for personnel people, is usually readable.

Many of the financial pages in the daily and weekly newspapers offer very good summaries of current issues; you should keep a watching brief on them.

Pensions Today is a shorter and gossipier read (£350, www. informafinance.com). The same publisher publishes the rather over-engineered The Pension Scheme Trustee £297.00. The PMI also publishes a newsletter (Trustee Group News, available from www.pensions-pmi.org.uk) which it distributes to its trustees group and is good value at £46.

The host of other periodicals, *Professional Pensions, Pensions Week, Pensions Management* and others are not really designed for trustees unless they are professional. A service as yet untested and unpriced is Hewitt Bacon & Woodrow's Trustee Online service (www.hewittbaconwoodrow.co.uk).

LAW

Textbooks. There is one major textbook, written by the author, called Pensions Law and Practice (Sweet and Maxwell looseleaf, four volumes, ISBN 042179190X, about £420). Whilst well-printed, and looking impressive on the bookshelf, it may be a little intimidating for everyday use. For the trust technician, *Sweet and Maxwell's Law of Occupational Pension Schemes* (Nigel Inglis-Jones, Sweet & Maxwell £445, ISBN 0421358408) is handy.

Equity and Trusts. If you are fascinated by the law of trusts and their history, skip most of the conventional texts. A readable, though long book, available in paperback, is Graham Moffat, *Trusts law: Texts and Materials*, Butterworths, £29.95 ISBN: 0406983801, 1999.

The standard book is *Underbill & Hayton: Law Relating to Trusts and Trustees*, 2002, Butterworths ISBN: 0406938849, £295. And, if you don't like this handbook, you could try a very different approach: Roger Self, *Tolley's Pension Fund Trustee Handbook*, £29,95, 2002 Tolley Publishing; ISBN: 0754516482.

Law Reports. You should not need to read law reports; if you are keen you can suggest your manager might take them, and your lawyer should certainly subscribe to them (Pensions Benefits Law Reports, Pensionslaw, www.pensionslaw.com). There are also two (at least) other series, *Pensions Law Reports*, (www.incomesdata.co.uk/pensions/penlaw.htm) and *Occupational Pensions Law Reports Pensions* (http://www.irseclipse. co.uk,) which follow the standard format.

Tax. You need to be a Senior Wrangler to understand the current tax structure of pension schemes. Fortunately as a trustee you really only need to know that they exist – and that most of them are to be abolished if the Inland Revenue paper published in December 2002 is implemented. Many of the rules (as well as the proposals for their abolition) are published in the Inland Revenue Practice Notes and occasional updates, available on the Inland Revenue website (www.inlandrevenue.gov.uk).

Social Security. You cannot be serious if you want to refer to the social security law; if you must, try *The Blue Volumes, Volume 5 (The Law Relating to Occupational Schemes*, http://www.dwp .gov.uk/advisers/docs/lawvols/bluevol/index.htm).

Statues. The amount of raw pensions law has increased over the last 20 years from about 40 pages to about 6,000 pages. Paper is now all but useless (although there are services) to cope with the complexity, although this publisher is publishing a one-volume guide; the full text in all its incomprehensible complexity is available on the incomparable *Perspective* (www.pendragon.co.uk) whose website which how much new stuff is published every day. A somewhat less sophisticated service is available on www.pensionspro.com. Both the services are subscriber only.

Surpluses and Deficits. A technical guide, rather than a policy review, is Philip Bennett's *Pension Fund Surpluses* (Sweet and Maxwell, 1994 2nd ed, ISBN 075200 0128 £86.50); as yet there is nothing quite as good on dealing with deficits. In any event the law is about to change on deficits and surpluses so it is a moving target.

THE PENSION SYSTEM

General. There are innumerable guides to the pensions system. One of the more practical is *Allied Dunbar Pensions Guide* Allied Dunbar Pensions Handbook, Anthony Reardon £27.99, 434 pages (2001), Financial Times Prentice Hall; ISBN: 0273654926 though a little technical. For the company secretary, try *Pensions (Good Practice)*, Andrew Scrimshaw, Paperback, 79 pp (2001) Chartered Institute of Personnel and Development (CIPD); ISBN: 0852929293 £13.99 and *Pensions Simplified*, Tony Granger, Richard Batemen £12.99 Paperback, 138 pp (2000) Management Books 2000; ISBN: 1852523271. See also *The Life Assurance and Pensions Handbook*, Chris Marshall, Price: £57.00.Paperback, 600 pp 2002, Taxbriefs Ltd ISBN: 1902824555.

Insurance Policies. There is no shortage of works on which is the best insurance contract; unfortunately none of them will tell you which will be the best policy in twenty-five years' time. Figures are published monthly in *Money Management*, and independent financial advisers have access to computer based systems – and the Financial Services Authority is supposed to be publishing a comparative survey on the web (www.fsa.gov.uk).

Jargon. The jargon of pensions is legion. You could try *Pensions terminology – A Glossary for Pension Schemes*, published by the Pensions Management Institute. 6th ed 2002 ISBN 1904120059 £8.00.

International. If you think it's bad in Britain, it's worth looking sometimes at what happens in the rest of the world. Always as up to date as these things can be is the *Introduction to Mercer's Worldwide Benefit and Employment Guidelines*, once free but now $4,000 pa! (www.mercerhr.com).

Employment policy. A rather tendentious consideration of the legal system and its involvement with pension is Richard Nobles' *Pensions, Employment and the Law* (Oxford Monographs on Labour Law, £55 hardback, ISBN 0-19-825448-2, Clarendon Press 1993).

ACCOUNTING

The impact of FRS 17 the rather naively drafted standard set by the accountancy profession for the disclosure of pensions obligations on the accounts of companies, has concentrated the minds of many companies on the pension issues; it is proving rather a disaster and with luck may well be abolished. It can be a technical area, but, if you want to avoid being outbluffed, one of the most useful guides is Accounts and Audit of Pension Schemes, Jo Rodgers £65.00 Paperback 2002, Butterworths Tolley; ISBN: 0406948038.

INVESTMENT

Investment is the fun part of being a trustee. A simple guide is *Pension Fund Investment* (Colin Lever & David Hager, Butterworths, 1989 ISBN 0-406-50052, pb). A somewhat technical approach to the law of investments is set out in *Law of Pension Fund Investment* (John Quarrell, 1990, Butterworths, ISBN 0-406-67819-7). More general and useful is *Pension Fund Investment* (A G Shepherd, Woodhead-Faulkner, 1987, ISBN 0-85941-400-0). There is also a series of guides on different investments in the 'Made Simple' series issued by the National Association of Pension Funds (www.napf.co.uk). See also Russell Sparkes, *Socially Responsible Investment – a Practical Guide for Professional Investors*, £24.95 Hardcover – 422 pp 2002 John Wiley and Sons Ltd; ISBN: 0471499536 and *Mark Mansley Socially Responsible Investment: a Guide for Pension Funds and Institutional Investors* £45.00 Paperback – 280 pp 2000, Monitor Press; ISBN: 187124191X.

POLICY

If you are interested in examining why pensions systems are so complicated you might like to look at some of the government papers on certain problems. The latest (2003) were published at the end of December 2002, *Simplicity, security and choice: working and saving for retirement* Is a Green paper with a shoal of accompanying documents – including a proposal for a radical simplification of the tax system. The Politics of Pension Reform: Institutions and Policy Change in Western Europe Giuliano Bonoli £12.95 Paperback 198 pages (14 September, 2000 Cambridge University Press; ISBN: 0521776066. A little bit over the top, and with a political agenda, but an easy read is Robin Blackburn, *Banking on Death: The Uses and Misuses of Pensions Funds* £20.00 Hardcover – 560 pages (March 2001) Verso Books; ISBN: 1859847951. The most influential book in recent years is World Bank, *Averting the Old Age Crisis: Policies to Protect the Old and Promote Growth* (World Bank Research Publications) £18.68 Paperback – 426 pages (1 November, 1994) Oxford University Press Inc, USA; ISBN: 0195209966.

Mergers and Acquisitions. The now defunct Occupational Pensions Board published a series of readable reports several years ago. Its final report, on what happens to pension funds on takeovers and mergers, and why there should be a pensions tribunal, was called *Protecting Pensions (Department of Social Security, Protecting Pensions: Safeguarding Benefits in a Changing Environment*, February 1989, The Stationery Office Books, 101pp, Cm 573, ISBN 0-10-105732-6, £8.30). See also Pensions Issues in Mergers and Acquisitions (Pensions Reports) Andrew and Punter, Jonathan White £102.95 Hardcover – 128 pages 1996 Sweet & Maxwell; ISBN: 0752002937.

A wider view is set out in Gordon L. Clark *European Pensions and Global Finance* £55.00 Hardcover – 250 pages 2003 Oxford University Press; ISBN: 0199253633.

Equal Treatment. A superb analysis of the problems of equal treatment is the House of Lords' Social Services Committee *Report on the Age of Retirement* (HCP3 1981-2). For a beautiful discussion (literally) of the problem of rationalising the state pension age, see *Options for Equality in State Pension Age*, (DSS, 1991, The Stationery Office, Cm 1723, ISBN 0-10-117232-X, £9.80). Now that retirement pension ages are to be abolished (by 2007) they are both an intriguing read.

Demography. There is a huge literature on 'whither pensions'; some of the more readable include: *Workers Versus Pensions: Intergenerational Justice in an Ageing World* (edited by Paul Johnson and others, Manchester University Press, 1989, ISBN 0-7190-3038-2, £); if you want to know how pensioners feel, read the spoof *The Thoughts of Pensioner Activist and Radical Granny Betty Spital*, (Christopher Meade, Penguin, 1989, ISBN 0-14-012150-1, £); the Organisation for Economic Co-operation and Development has produced *Ageing Populations: The Social Policy Implications* (OECD, from HMSO, 1988, ISBN 92-64-131123-2, now out of print, which is much shorter, 99pp – by 2040 the proportion of people over 65 will have doubled. The classic work is James H. Schulz *The Economics of Aging* : £21.50 Paperback – 360 pages 2000 Auburn House; ISBN: 0865692955; and the standard guide is now Richard Disney and Paul Johnson, *Pension Systems and*

Retirement Outcomes Across OECD Countries £65.00 Hardcover – 384 pages 2001, Edward Elgar; ISBN: 1840645636.

The Pensions System. If you would like to read background papers on the reform of the pension system in 1986 and later, it was all set out in what became known as The Fowler Report (in homage to the Beveridge Report half-a-century before); in some ways it foresaw the mess we are now in *Reform of Social Security* (3 vols, Cmnd 9517, 9518, 9519, 1985, ISBN 0-10-195170-1, 0-10-195180-9, ISBN 0-10-195190-6, £3.00 for the first volume, The Stationery Office) A bizarre and very personal approach was set out in *Pensions and Privilege: How to end the scandal, simplify taxes and widen ownership* (Philip Chappell, Centre for Policy Studies, 8 Wilfred Street, London SW1E 6PL, 1988, ISBN 1-870-265-23-8) which attacked company pension schemes in rather intemperate language. It is interesting to read, to see how some of the ideas proposed there (eg personal pensions) have now come to grief.

Reform. There's nothing to beat The Goode Report *(Pension Law Reform)* which is a classic of its kind – easy reading and a brilliant survey of the current situation, although now we know that its belief that a new law can remedy wrongs was somewhat naïve (Cm 2342-1, The Stationery Office Books, September 1993 £50.00).

DIVORCE

There are two main texts, both heavy going: one is Ellison & Rae, Family Breakdown and Pensions, Butterworths, 2002 £45.00 Paperback – 330 pages Butterworths; ISBN: 0406913102; the other is David Salter, *Pensions and Insurance on Family Breakdown* £45.00 Hardcover – 450 pages (2003) Family Law; ISBN: 0853086982.

Trade Unions. There are unfortunately at present few suitable
guides to trade union practice in pensions, although the TUC
pensions department and certain leading unions, provide an
excellent service to members. A partisan view was set out some
years ago in *The Essential Guide to Pensions: A Worker's
Handbook*, (Sue Ward, Pluto Press, 1988, ISBN 1-85305-093-8). But
there is nothing current on the topic; best bet is to browse the TUC
website occasionally (www.tuc.org.uk.).

SOCIAL SECURITY

Social security and its impact on pensions is a minefield. The
standard guide is Kate Tonge Tolley's *Social Security and State
Benefits: A Practical Guide*, £40.00 Paperback, 2002) Tolley
Publishing; ISBN: 0754516571.

State Benefits. The most useful guides in practice are on the
DWP website www.dwp.gov.uk.

COMMUNICATION

One of the undervalued areas of pensions, marketing your scheme,
is a crucial social service. There is nothing current on the subject,
but if you can find a copy, a useful, simple and well-written guide,
setting out sample booklets and newsletters is *Pensions: Promoting
and Communicating Your Scheme* (by Sue Ward, published by the
Industrial Society Press, 1990, ISBN 0-85290-472-X).

STATISTICS

Getting statistics in pensions is rarely a problem – getting useful
ones is all but impossible. The government (National Statistics)
publishes a wide range of pensions statistics on http://www
.statistics.gov.uk and UBS publish *Pension Fund Indicators*
analysing investments. The NAPF publishes an annual survey which
shows what pension funds are doing now in certain abstruse areas

– but fails to show trends or comparative figures. You can use their database by arrangement. A useful guide, really designed for use by actuaries, is the *Pensions Pocketbook*, which comes out every year (NTC Publications/Bacon & Woodrow, Farm Road, Henley on Thames, Oxfordshire RG9 1EJ (01491 574671), £26). £26.00 Paperback NTC Publications; ISBN: 1841160458. The Government Actuary's Department website shows the state of play on surveys of occupational schemes (www.gad.gov.uk).

Watsons Statistics is a nicely produced monthly digest of pensions statistics (Watson Wyatt Worldwide, www.watsonwyatt.com/europe).

Directories. The NAPF publishes a yearbook (NAPF, NIOC House, 4 Victoria Street, London SW1H 0NE (020 7808 1300) www.napf.co.uk) and the principle directory is *Pension Funds and their Advisers* (Alan Phillipp, AP Information Services Ltd, Marlborough House, 298 Regents Park Road, London N3 2UU 020 8349 9988 £250 www.ap-info.co.uk). They also publish *People in Pensions*. Local authority trustees (councillors and others) should have the *PIRC Local Authority Pension Fund Yearbook*, (annual, PIRC, ISBN 0-904677-42-7, £205 www.pirc.co.uk).

Investments. There is no good all round guide; however, *Pension Fund Indicators* is published annually by UBS Global Asset Management and gives a survey of the various sectors with good graphs and charts (sometimes over-complicated). www.ubs.com/e/globalam_uk/publications.html. (Free.)

Comparative Surveys. If you are asked to compare benefits in your scheme with other schemes, you can commission a survey of your own surprisingly cheaply – the NAPF will run a search through its database, though you won't know the names of the other companies.

MANAGEMENT AND ADMINISTRATION

There do not, as yet, appear to be any useful guides to administration and management. All the former titles all now seem to be out of print.

GIVING ADVICE

By and large, the message is don't, except as indicated in Chapter 21. But if you are asked for a guide try the 'Which?' *Guide to Planning Your Pensions: How to Maximize Your Retirement Income* (Which? Consumer Guides) Jonquil Lowe £10.99 Paperback – 336 pages (25 July, 2002) Which? Books; ISBN: 0852029012.

APPENDIX VII

THE NAPF CHECKLIST FOR PENSION FUND TRUSTEES

(Reproduced by kind permission of the National Association of Pension Funds)

1 Constitution of the Scheme

- Are you satisfied that the Trust Deed and Rules are fully up to date and implemented in full?

- Is your own appointment and that of your fellow trustees in order and in accordance with the Trust Deed and Rules?

- Is there provision for an independent trustee? If not, should there be?

2 Investments

- Are the arrangements for managing the assets adequate?

- Are the investment managers independent of the company? If not, are there adequate safeguards?

- Are the powers of investment managers clearly defined?

- Are the classes of investment controlled? (eg authorised, not unduly risky)

- Is self-investment permitted? Does it happen? Is there a policy for phasing it out?
- Does the fund participate in a performance measurement service?

3 Security of Assets

- Are there adequate arrangements for custody of scheme assets?

- Is there a separate custodian trustee? If not, should there be?

- Is there a separate bank account for the scheme?

- Do the procedures for authorising transfers of cash and assets provide sufficient safeguards?

- Are bank mandates appropriate and lists of signatories up to date?

4 Financial Control

- Are scheme auditors properly appointed?

- Are there any qualifications to the last audited accounts?

- Are payments of employers' and employees' contributions received regularly and on time?

- Are payments of benefits subject to adequate checks? (eg birth certificates, death certificates etc)

- Are internal audits or other checks conducted between annual audits?

- Are trustee meetings held often enough? Do you attend them?

5 Information to Scheme Members

- When you are satisfied that the arrangements for your scheme are adequate, would it be helpful to write to scheme members to reassure them?

6 Action Programme

- If the answer to any of the above questions is unsatisfactory, what action needs to be taken to remedy the matter?

NAPF, December 1991

APPENDIX VIII

THE PENSIONS YEAR

The Pensions Year is full of luscious conferences all over the world. It is a poor trustee that cannot get himself invited on one of more of these jollys – and as part of the training that trustees nowadays should undergo, it is not as cynical an exercise as might seem. If you have members in other parts of the world, you might as well look at some of the overseas conference, some of which are free or nearly free. The UK spends relatively little on training; but considering the sums you are responsible for, and the future comfort of all those pensioners (of whom you may be one) a little training is not so terrible, and very cost-effective. You should also agree to send the scheme manager on one or two, particularly in the South of France.

Who does the training? As well as the institutions (the NAPF, the PMI and others) many commercial organisations run training sessions. The actuarial and pensions consultancies run many useful ones, but with less emphasis on your legal obligations and you may end up knowing more about actuarial science than you really need. The commercial training conferences only spasmodically run courses, and usually on more specialised topics; they are also expensive. If there are enough of you, get your solicitor to come in and give you an afternoon of his time. It will usually be cheaper and more fun, as well as more useful.

JANUARY

Some useful, commercially-run, conferences are marketed in January. You can ask to be placed on the mailing lists of the principal ones (including Tolley Conferences, Tolley House, 2 Addiscombe Road, Croydon, Surrey CR9 5AF, 0181-686 9141, IBC, Fourth Floor, 57/61 Mortimer Street, London W1N 7TD, 020 7637 4383, and Hawksmere, 12-18 Grosvenor Gardens, London SW1W 0DH, 020 7824 8257)

FEBRUARY

The NAPF Investment Conference is a real eye-opener, especially when the property guys are there – the car park is jammed with Ferraris, most of them paid for by you. The recession does not seem to have affected the car fleet much. The bad news is that it is in Eastbourne, which can be bitterly cold and miserable. The hotel is improving by the year.

MARCH

The Budget usually contains something about pensions, including any increase in state benefits and changes to National Insurance contributions.

APRIL

The NAPF Annual Conference is a must for at least one of you, to find out what are the problems over the next year or two, pick up a few tips, see what is on offer at the exhibition, and just keep a feel on the industry. There is no shortage of free alcohol. If you have a tendency to bulkiness, you might need to book into a health farm the following week.

AUGUST

Like France, the Pensions Industry is on holiday, and so should you be.

SEPTEMBER

Still on holiday.

OCTOBER

The PMI Autumn Conference, always well attended, and generally not too technical. Good value.

NOVEMBER

The NAPF holds an annual Autumn Conference for just one day. A summary of latest developments. An occasional visit is enough.

DECEMBER

December is the month for investment managers' and stockbrokers' parties. Some of these can be very good indeed, although if you have a split fund (see Bluffer's Guide) you might get sick of the sight of turkey. Other than that, there are very few pensions conferences.

Qualifications and Training

Trustee training is a sensible use of precious time; but you need the right course. You need to decide whether you want training:

- on how pension schemes work (offered by most of the consultants and actuaries) or

- on trustee responsibilities and obligations – much more difficult to find.

The Trustee Certificate

The *Pensions Management Institute* (see Addresses) offers a Fellowship and Associateship in pensions management (FPMI and APMI) and now has a more basic qualification for junior administrators called the Qualification in Pensions Administration (QPA). They offer a qualification in trusteeship with a certificate available. There are internal politics to resolve if all members undertake to take the examination; it would look unfortunate if a member-nominated trustee qualified and the chairman did not; and if he failed, what would that say about the calibre of his trusteeship! The examination is somewhat slanted towards making a trustee a form of semi-consultant, rather than a trustee, so don't feel too worried if you find it inappropriate.

Associations

Very good value is provided by the PMI Trustee Group (see Pensions Management Institute, Addresses) with a regular newsletter (PMI Trustee Group News) and access to meetings and training. The annual fee is £45, plus a 20% discount when three or more members enrol together.

The *TUC Member Trustees' Network* (TUC Congress House, Great Russell Street, London WC1B 3LS) offers a specialist service for member-nominated trustees, which also provides a copy of the

TUC Trustee News, TUC trustee training services, guidance notes on electing member trustees and the conduct of trustee meetings and information about pension fund investment. It clearly adopts a particular approach, but it offers a useful service.

IRS Training run an occasional course, using practising pensions lawyers (IRS Training, 18-20 Highbury Place, London N5 1QP, around £260 + VAT).

The *National Association of Pension Funds* (see Addresses) also offers good value courses taking a couple of days, but depend very much on who is doing the teaching – they recruit from the industry, which is good, but not all experts are good teachers. It publishes a short guide 'Trusteeship made simple' (8pp).

Hawksmere (12-18 Grosvenor Gardens, London SW1W OBD 020 7824 8257) offers specialist trustee training, either on a group basis, or designed for individual funds.

Consultants and others also run training on an ad hoc basis; there are lists of these courses published occasionally in *Pensions World*.

PENALTIES FOR TRUSTEES

The following chart looks, at first glance, formidable and intimidating. And indeed, if the penalties were ever imposed for every tiny breach, being a trustee would be a mug's game. Fortunately, OPRA has made it clear that they are not to be a nit-picking regulator, and in real life it is highly unlikely that any of these penalties would be imposed other than in the case of fraud or flagrant disregard of a warning from OPRA. It would bring the whole system of regulation into disrepute if, as one distinguished observer noted, trustees were fined £5,000 per breach of an obligation to take a note of the time of their trustees' meetings every month for a year (ie £60,000 per trustee), yet the trustees of another scheme, who were meticulous about minute-taking but more cavalier about ownership of the assets, would be, because the burden of proof is greater in criminal matters, acquitted of fraud.

In practice, therefore, there is nothing to fear. But just in case...

Regulatory Breaches

No.	Matter	Breach	Penalty	Reference	Commentary/ how to avoid liability
Prohibition order only under PA95 s3 (by OPRA)					
1	Scheme registration	Serious or persistent breach of a duty concerning	Prohibition as a trustee	PA95 s3(2)	
2	Transfer values	Serious or persistent breach of a duty concerning	Prohibition as a trustee	PA95 s3(2)	
3	Disclosure	Serious or persistent breach of a duty concerning	Prohibition as a trustee	PA95 s3(2)	
4	Levy	Serious or persistent breach of a duty concerning	Prohibition as a trustee	PA95 s3(2)	
5	Leaving excess assets on a winding-up	Failure to take reasonable steps to distribute assets in accordance with PA95	Prohibition as a trustee	PA95 s77(5)	
6	Recovery of any assets of value to the extent possible without disproportionate cost when an application is made to the Pension Compensation Scheme	Failure to take reasonable steps	Prohibition as a trustee	PA95 s81(6)	

No.	Matter	Breach	Penalty	Reference	Commentary/ how to avoid liability
7	Disqualifi-cation of an actuary or auditor to the scheme as trustee		Prohibition as a trustee	PA95 s28(4)	

Civil fine only under PA95 s10 (maximum £5,000 per individual, £50,000 per company; lower maxima in certain cases prescribed by regulation)

No.	Matter	Breach	Penalty	Reference	Commentary/ how to avoid liability
8	Dispute resolution procedure	Failure to take reasonable steps to secure	Civil fine	PA95 s50(6)	
9	Statement of guaranteed entitlement to a transfer value to a member of the scheme within the prescribed time	Failure to take reasonable steps to supply	Civil fine	PA95 s153(4)	

Prohibition order and/or civil fine under PA95 s3 and s10

No.	Matter	Breach	Penalty	Reference	Commentary/ how to avoid liability
10	Failure by the employer to pay benefits	Failure to take reasonable steps to comply with a direction from OPRA	Prohibition order/ civil fine	PA95 s15(4)	
11	Statement drafted by OPRA for insertion in annual report	Failure to take reasonable steps to publish	Prohibition order/ civil fine	PA95 s15(4)	
12	Copy of a statement prepared by OPRA	Failure to take reasonable steps to send members	Prohibition order/ civil fine	PA95 s15(4)	

No.	Matter	Breach	Penalty	Reference	Commentary/ how to avoid liability
13	Member-nominated trustees	Failure to take reasonable steps to comply with duty to implement arrangements for selection	Prohibition order/ civil fine	PA95 s21(1),(2)	
14	Scheme assets not to be used to indemnify trustees for fines or civil penalties	Failure to take reasonable steps to ensure	Prohibition order/ civil fine	PA95 s31(3)	
15	Trustee meeting where a decision is to be taken by majority voting	Failure to take reasonable steps to give proper notice	Prohibition order/ civil fine	PA95 s32(5)	
16	Written statement of investment principles	Failure to take reasonable steps to prepare	Prohibition order/ civil fine	PA95 s35(6)	
17	Failure to take and consider written advice before preparing a statement of investment principles		Prohibition order/ civil fine	PA95 s35(6)	

No.	Matter	Breach	Penalty	Reference	Commentary/ how to avoid liability
18	Failure to take reasonable steps to obtain professional advice in choosing the scheme investments		Prohibition order/ civil fine	PA95 s36(8)	
19	Making a payment out of surplus to the employer without taking reasonable steps to comply with the requirements		Prohibition order/ civil fine	PA95 s37(8)	
20	Failure to take reasonable steps to observe restrictions on self-investment in relation to employer-related investments		Prohibition order/ civil fine	PA95 s40(4)	

No.	Matter	Breach	Penalty	Reference	Commentary/ how to avoid liability
21	Placing reliance on an adviser who has not been appointed by the trustees		Prohibition order/ civil fine	PA95 s47(3)	including examination of/ expression of opinion on accounts; questions on financial funding and mortality; and custody SI 1996/1715 reg 2
22	Appointment of scheme auditor	Failure to take reasonable steps to appoint; failure to appoint in compliance with the requirements of the PA95	Prohibition order/ civil fine	PA95 s47(8)	not applicable to unfunded, unapproved, death benefit only, SSAS schemes SI 1996/1715 reg 3
23	Appointment of scheme actuary	Failure to take reasonable steps to appoint; failure to appoint in compliance with the requirements of the PA95	Prohibition order/ civil fine	PA95 s47(8)	
24	Appointment of scheme fund manager	Failure to take reasonable steps to appoint; failure to appoint in compliance with the requirements of the PA95	Prohibition order/ civil fine	PA95 s47(8)	
25	Information to scheme's professional advisers	Failure to take reasonable steps to disclose	Prohibition order/ civil fine	PA95 s47(11)	

No.	Matter	Breach	Penalty	Reference	Commentary/ how to avoid liability
26	Requirement to operate a separate bank account	Failure to take reasonable steps to comply	Prohibition order/ civil fine	PA95 s49(6)	
27	Requirement to keep records of meetings	Failure to take reasonable steps to comply	Prohibition order/ civil fine	PA95 s49(6)	
28	Requirement to keep specified books and records	Failure to take reasonable steps to comply	Prohibition order/ civil fine	PA96 s49(6)	
29	Duties under minimum funding requirement	Failure to take reasonable steps to comply	Prohibition order/ civil fine	PA95 s57(7)	
30	Preparation of schedule of contributions under minimum funding requirement	Failure to take reasonable steps to comply with duty	Prohibition order/ civil fine	PA95 s58(8)	
31	Maintenance of schedule of contributions under minimum funding requirement	Failure to take reasonable steps to comply with duty	Prohibition order/ civil fine	PA95 s58(8)	

No.	Matter	Breach	Penalty	Reference	Commentary/ how to avoid liability
32	Revision of schedule of contributions under minimum funding requirement	Failure to take reasonable steps to comply with duty	Prohibition order/ civil fine	PA95 s58(8)	
33	Informing OPRA that contributions required under the schedule of contributions have not been paid by due date	Failure to take reasonable steps to inform	Prohibition order/ civil fine	PA95 s59(4)	
34	Informing the members of the scheme that contributions required under the schedule of contributions have not been paid by due date	Failure to take reasonable steps to inform	Prohibition order/ civil fine	PA95 s59(4)	
35	Informing OPRA that minimum funding requirement not met	Failure to take reasonable steps to inform	Prohibition order/ civil fine	PA95 s59(4)	

No.	Matter	Breach	Penalty	Reference	Commentary/ how to avoid liability
36	Informing the members of the scheme that minimum funding requirement not met	Failure to take reasonable steps to inform	Prohibition order/ civil fine	PA95 s59(4)	
37	Informing OPRA that the employer has not restored the scheme's funding to at least 90% of the minimum funding requirement within the required period	Failure to take reasonable steps to inform	Prohibition order/ civil fine	PA95 s60(8)	
38	Informing the members of the scheme that the employer has not restored the scheme's funding to at least 90% of the minimum funding requirement within the required period	Failure to take reasonable steps to inform	Prohibition order/ civil fine	PA95 s60(8)	

No.	Matter	Breach	Penalty	Reference	Commentary/ how to avoid liability
39	Winding-up the scheme and order of priorities for satisfying liabilities	Failure to take reasonable steps to comply with the requirements	Prohibition order/ civil fine	PA95 s73(6)	
40	Distributing assets to employer on a winding-up	Failure to take reasonable steps to comply with requirements	Prohibition order/ civil fine	PA95 s76(6)	
41	Prepare a payment schedule for a money purchase scheme	Failure to take reasonable steps to comply	Prohibition order/ civil fine	PA95 s87(5)	
42	Maintain a payment schedule for a money purchase scheme	Failure to take reasonable steps to comply	Prohibition order/ civil fine	PA95 s87(5)	Money purchase scheme only
43	Revise a payment schedule for a money purchase scheme	Failure to take reasonable steps to comply	Prohibition order/ civil fine	PA95 s87(5)	

No.	Matter	Breach	Penalty	Reference	Commentary/ how to avoid liability
44	Informing OPRA when any contributions listed on the payment schedule for a money purchase scheme have not been paid by the due date	Failure to take reasonable steps to inform	Prohibition order/ civil fine	PA95 s88(4)	
45	Informing the members when any contributions listed on the payment schedule for a money purchase scheme have not been paid by the due date	Failure to take reasonable steps to inform	Prohibition order/ civil fine	PA95 s88(4)	

Criminal offences (on indictment, maximum 2 years prison and/or unlimited fine; on summary conviction, fine level 1-5)

No.	Matter	Breach	Penalty	Reference	Commentary
46	Acting as trustee while prohibited or suspended by OPRA		Maximum 2 years prison and /or unlimited fine	PA95 s6(1)	
47	Acting as auditor while serving as a trustee or connected with a trustee		Maximum 2 years prison and /or unlimited fine	PA95 s28(1)	

No.	Matter	Breach	Penalty	Reference	Commentary/ how to avoid liability
48	Acting as actuary while serving as a trustee or connected with a trustee		Maximum 2 years prison and /or unlimited fine	PA95 s28(1)	
49	Acting as a trustee while an actuary to the scheme		Maximum 2 years prison and /or unlimited fine	PA95 s28(1)	
50	Acting as trustee while an auditor to the scheme		Maximum 2 years prison and /or unlimited fine	PA95 s28(1)	
51	Acting as trustee while disqualified		Maximum 2 years prison and /or unlimited fine	PA95 s30(3)	
52	Reimburse-ment by fund of fines or civil penalties		Maximum 2 years prison and /or unlimited fine	PA95 s31(5)	
53	Investing fund assets in the employer over the self-invest-ment limits		Maximum 2 years prison and /or unlimited fine	PA95 s40(5)	

No.	Matter	Breach	Penalty	Reference	Commentary/ how to avoid liability
54	Intentionally delaying an OPRA inspector	Without reasonable excuse	Maximum 2 years prison and /or unlimited fine (summary: level 5)	PA95 s101(2)(a)	
55	Neglects or refuses to produce a document required by OPRA inspector	Without reasonable excuse	Maximum 2 years prison and /or unlimited fine (summary: level 5)	PA95 s101(2)(b)	
56	Neglects or refuses to answer a question or to provide information required by OPRA inspector	Without reasonable excuse	Maximum 2 years prison and /or unlimited fine (summary: level 5)	PA95 s101(2)(c)	
57	Knowingly or recklessly provides OPRA with false or misleading information	Where to an OPRA inspector or in course of OPRA business	Maximum 2 years prison and /or unlimited fine (summary: statutory maximum)	PA95 s101(5)	
58	Alters, suppresses conceals or destroys any document required to be produced to OPRA	Intentionally and without reasonable excuse	Maximum 2 years prison and /or unlimited fine (summary: statutory maximum)	PA95 s101(6)	

No.	Matter	Breach	Penalty	Reference	Commentary/ how to avoid liability
59	Discloses restricted information obtained by OPRA		Maximum 2 years prison and /or unlimited fine (summary: statutory maximum)	PA95 s104(1)	
60	Neglects or refuses to produce a document required by the Pensions Compensation Board	Without reasonable excuse	Maximum 2 years prison and /or unlimited fine (summary: level 5)	PA95 s111(1)	
61	Provides the Pensions Compensation Board with false or misleading information	Knowingly or recklessly	Maximum 2 years prison and /or unlimited fine (summary: statutory maximum)	PA95 s111(4)	
62	Alters, suppresses conceals or destroys any document required to be produced to the Pensions Compensation Board	Intentionally and without reasonable excuse	Maximum 2 years prison and /or unlimited fine (summary: statutory maximum)	PA95 s111(5)	
63	Breaches regulations under PSA93 (to be expanded)		Fine not exceeding level 5	PSA93 s168	

No.	Matter	Breach	Penalty	Reference	Commentary/ how to avoid liability
64	Provides Pensions Registrar with information which is false or misleading	Knowingly or recklessly	Maximum 2 years prison and /or unlimited fine (summary: statutory maximum)	PSA93 s168A	

APPENDIX X

CHECKLIST FOR COMPLIANCE

No.	Duty	Reference	Method of compliance	Comment
1	Check with OPRA Register whether any trustees (or director of disqualified company) have been disqualified		Secretary to write to OPRA informing of intention to appoint new trustee	
2	Check whether scheme's actuary, auditor, undischarged bankrupt (or undischarged arrangement with creditors) or DTI disqualified company director or company in liquidation			
3	Statement of investment principles: advice		1. Ask actuary to prepare letter of advice, and file with minutes 2. Ensure minutes record discussion 3. Send copy of letter to fund manager	

No.	Duty	Reference	Method of compliance	Comment
4	Statement of investment principles: preparation		Ask investment adviser or actuary to prepare statement; record discussion and if necessary amendment; keep copy with minutes; confirm copy with investment advisers	
5	Dispute resolution		Ask solicitors to ensure simple system built into trust deed	
6	Minimum funding		Actuary to ensure compliance	
7	Contributions collection		Ensure administrator (in administration agreement) required to report any failure to pay	
8	Quorum for meeting	SI 1996/1715 reg 9	Ensure quorum for meeting	
9	Notice for meeting	SI 1996/1715 reg10	Manner of and time for giving notice when specified number of trustees must be present for meeting	
10	Bank account	SI 1996/1715 reg 11; PA95 s49(1)	Separate bank account to be kept by trustees	

No.	Duty	Reference	Method of compliance	Comment
11	Books and records	SI 1996/1715 reg 12	1. Keep records of meetings 2. Books and records of amount of any contribution; date when member joins scheme; payments of pensions and benefits; payments to any person including professional advisers and reason why; movement or transfer of assets in or out of scheme; where transfer, the date, amount, terms, name of other scheme 3. Name of insurer and date purchased of any policies 4. Payments made to employer 5. Other payments	In practice, administrator will carry out all this – but trustees should check the minutes. Delegate all other duties to administrator under contract.
12	Trustee minutes	SI 1996/1715 reg 13; PA 95 s49(4)	Date time and place of meeting; names of all trustees invited; names of those who attended and those who did not; names of professional advisers and any other person who attended; any decisions made; whether since previous meeting any decision made by trustees, and if so time place and date and the names of trustees who participated.	
13	Period of records	SI 1996/1715 reg 14	Keep records for 6 years after end of scheme year	

No.	Duty	Reference	Method of compliance	Comment
14	Employer payments	SI 1996/1715 reg 15	Employer must pay into bank benefits received (eg from insurer) into trust account if not paid over	
15	Contributions monitoring	SI 1996/1715 reg 16	Trustees must check that deductions by employer from employees' salaries to pension scheme have been paid over within 14 days from end of month; must notify OPRA within 30 days of breach and members within 90 days.	

Thorogood publishing

Thorogood publishes a wide range of books, reports, special briefings, psychometric tests and videos. Listed below is a selection of key titles.

Desktop Guides

The marketing strategy desktop guide   *Norton Paley* • £16.99

The sales manager's desktop guide
                                   Mike Gale and Julian Clay • £16.99

The company director's desktop guide   *David Martin* • £16.99

The credit controller's desktop guide   *Roger Mason* • £16.99

The company secretary's desktop guide   *Roger Mason* • £16.99

The finance and accountancy desktop guide *Ralph Tiffin* • £16.99

The commercial engineer's desktop guide   *Tim Boyce* • £16.99

The training manager's desktop guide   *Eddie Davies* • £16.99

The PR practitioner's desktop guide   *Caroline Black* • £16.99

Win new business – the desktop guide   *Susan Croft* • £16.99

Masters in Management

Mastering business planning and strategy   *Paul Elkin* • £19.99

Mastering financial management   *Stephen Brookson* • £19.99

Mastering leadership   *Michael Williams* • £19.99

Mastering marketing   *Ian Ruskin-Brown* • £22.00

Mastering negotiations   *Eric Evans* • £19.99

Mastering people management   *Mark Thomas* • £19.99

Mastering personal and interpersonal skills
Peter Haddon • £16.99

Mastering project management   *Cathy Lake* • £19.99

Business Action Pocketbooks

Edited by David Irwin

Building your business pocketbook   £10.99

Developing yourself and your staff pocketbook   £10.99

Finance and profitability pocketbook   £10.99

Managing and employing people pocketbook   £10.99

Sales and marketing pocketbook   £10.99

Managing projects and operations pocketbook   £9.99

Effective business communications pocketbook   £9.99

PR techniques that work   *Edited by Jim Dunn* • £9.99

Adair on leadership   *Edited by Neil Thomas* • £9.99

Other titles

The John Adair handbook of management and leadership
Edited by Neil Thomas • £29.95

The inside track to successful management
Dr Gerald Kushel • £16.95

Boost your company's profits *Barrie Pearson • £12.99*

Negotiate to succeed *Julie Lewthwaite • £12.99*

The management tool kit *Sultan Kermally • £10.99*

Working smarter *Graham Roberts-Phelps • £15.99*

Test your management skills *Michael Williams • £12.99*

The art of headless chicken management
Elly Brewer and Mark Edwards • £6.99

EMU challenge and change – the implications for business
John Atkin • £11.99

Everything you need for an NVQ in management
Julie Lewthwaite • £19.99

Customer relationship management
Graham Roberts-Phelps • £12.99

Time management and personal development
John Adair and Melanie Allen • £9.99

Sales management and organisation *Peter Green • £9.99*

Telephone tactics *Graham Roberts-Phelps • £9.99*

Companies don't succeed people do!
Graham Roberts-Phelps • £12.99

Inspiring leadership *John Adair • £24.99*

The book of ME	*Barrie Pearson and Neil Thomas* • £24.99
The complete guide to debt recovery	*Roger Mason* • £12.99
Janner's speechmaker	*Greville Janner* • £12.99
Dynamic practice development	*Kim Tasso* • £29.99
Gurus on business strategy	*Tony Grundy* • £14.99

Thorogood also has an extensive range of reports and special briefings which are written specifically for professionals wanting expert information.

For a full listing of all Thorogood publications, or to order any title, please call Thorogood Customer Services on 020 7749 4748 or fax on 020 7729 6110. Alternatively, please view our website at **www.thorogood.ws**.